P9-EEF-630

HIGH TIMES BOOKS PRESENTS

PARENTS' GUIDE TO MARIJUANA

BY DR. MITCH EARLEYWINE
ILLUSTRATIONS BY STEVEN WACKSMAN

TABLE OF CONTENTS

Produced by HIGH TIMES BOOKS

FIRST EDITION: OCTOBER 2007

ISBN-13#:978-1-893010-24-6
ISBN-10#:1-893010-24-4
PRICE:$12.95

PRINTED IN CHINA

ACKNOWLEDGEMENTS

My hearty thanks to my usual support team that has helped me reach this far: Josh Gross, Jim DeSantis, Clark and Suzy Van Scoyk, Joe Earleywine, Mark Myers and Tamar Golan, Norman Miller and Vicki Pollock, Jack Huntington, David and Felice Gordis, Allen St. Pierre, Paul Armentano, Rob Kampia, Chuck Thomas, Marsha Rosenbaum, Ethan Nadelmann, Ethan Russo, Mary McEvoy, Natasha Lewin and Stanton Peele. Bob Earleywine went above and beyond on this one, reading every word that's here and many that didn't make it, and offering the kind of support any son dreams of. Bruce Mirken, one of the two men alive whom I'm willing to let touch my prose, was a genuine inspiration.

I enthusiastically thank all my old pals at the University of Southern California. A supreme thank you to all my new friends at the University at Albany, State University of New York. It's not easy hiring "Dr. Pot." Thanks for taking the gamble!

The folks at Trans-High Corporation have been utterly superb and I can't thank them all enough. Michael Kennedy has been a consistent, accepting, thoughtful and enthusiastic force behind this work. In truth, this book was his idea. I don't think I would've had the guts to write this one if he hadn't asked. He also forced me to take a stand on some issues I had hedged about in the past. Steve Bloom has been a dependable help and a superb model. (I think I learned how to use a semicolon from his blog.) Rick Cusick always kept me smiling and thinking; he still has the best Willie Nelson/Bob Dylan stories I have ever heard. David "Bean" Bienenstock, the other man alive whom I'm willing to let touch my prose, taught me to write better leads and loosen up. Steve Hager helped me trust my instincts with a simple story that began "I know this is true because my heart told it to my head...."

My daughters, Dahlia and Maya, continue to teach me new lessons every day. I hope that they can someday forgive me for spending time coaching other parents when those hours could have been spent with them. May they grow up in a land where the severity of punishments fits but never exceeds the severity of crimes! Elana Gordis continues to be the most perfect wife for me. I would elaborate, but I don't want to make other married men weep. Jack Black, Kyle Gass and Domenico Scarlatti offered more support than they might know. Special gratitude to Manny and Ida Slawin, Hattie Crumption, Dick Young and Robert Blinder. I also extend a loud and effusive "WOO!" to every student who has ever taken the infamous "Drug Class." You all taught me tons and tons.

But most of all, I thank every parent who takes the time to try to do it right. People without kids are never going to understand. We'll never be perfect, but we can always do our best to clean up our mistakes.

CHAPTER 1: GETTING THEM TO TALK ABOUT IT

I don't know how I get myself into these things, but there I was, standing before at least a dozen parents. Some were younger and some were older. Some were dressed up and some wore jeans. I was glad to see a bunch of fathers with the mothers. I asked everyone to move their chairs in a circle so it wouldn't feel like school. A few people smiled at that.

I introduced myself. As I often do when I'm nervous, I mentioned my Ph.D. and my previous book, *Understanding Marijuana*. I don't know if it helps parents think I'm qualified, but it calms me down a little. I asked for each person's name and some background about their children. I passed out name tags. We had a few couples and many who were there alone. They had sons and daughters of almost every age. Although most folks sounded a little guarded, we all agreed that parenting brought its difficult moments. Almost everyone mentioned rough times raising teens today.

"I don't understand why it's got to be so rough," said Ricardo, a tall man in a dress shirt and slacks to my right. "I don't remember giving my parents this much trouble."

"It was a different time then," said Christine. "So much is going on now that wasn't the case when we were kids."

"What can you tell us?" asked Ricardo. I think it was the question of the moment. Everyone else was probably wondering the same thing.

"All I can really do is two things. I can tell you the truth about marijuana so you'll know what's a fact and what's a myth. And I can talk about what helps parents build good relationships with teens. You'll have to see what works for you and discuss ways to fine-tune it," I said.

"Sounds reasonable," Ricardo said.

"Where would you like to start?" I asked.

"When do I start talking to my kids about drugs?" asked Ada, a dark-haired woman sitting to my left.

OPPORTUNITIES

"Let's jump right in," I said. "Can I tell you a story if I promise to keep it brief?" They all nodded. "My oldest daughter and I were listening to the radio. Janis Joplin came on, singing 'Piece of My Heart.'" The older parents nodded again. "My daughter asked, 'Is that a man or a woman singing?' I laughed and said that it was Janis Joplin, that she was a great performer, and she touched a lot of hearts."

"She also overdosed on heroin," said Alex, a blond man in a blue shirt and tie.

"Exactly," I said. "So I saw that this was a golden opportunity. I added, 'She did drugs that killed her; it's too bad.'"

"What did your daughter say?" Ada asked.

"She said, 'I'm not going to do drugs. I want to be an artist.' So I said, 'Good for you!'"

Ada gave me a friendly nod.

"How old was your daughter at the time?" she asked.

"Four. Four years old."

"That's pretty young! Why do you bother?" asked Sebastian, a curly-haired man to my right.

"I don't know," I said. "But when you write a book on marijuana, you worry. When she was 3 years old she pointed to the Canadian flag and said 'Marijuana!'"

They laughed.

I added, "I figured I better get to work if I wanted to keep her off drugs."

"Well, what else did you tell her?" Ada asked.

"Nothing right then. She wanted to talk about art. So that's what we did. But I think I planted a little seed. That's what these golden opportunities are about."

"I doubt that one little chat is going to keep her off drugs," Alex blurted. "I mean, no offense."

"I agree," I said. "But little chances like that come up a lot. If I had turned it into a big lecture, she would have tuned out. Don't you think?"

"Absolutely," said Stephanie, a brown-haired woman with glasses sitting directly across from me. Other parents nodded.

"More opportunities show up every week, though. Sometimes there's a marijuana story on TV. Sometimes something relevant is on the radio. I'll see something in a newspaper. Then I get a chance to ask her about it and maybe put my two cents in." Everyone nodded.

"It sounds good right now, but I don't know what to say at the moment," said Ada. People nodded in agreement.

"I try not to do so much of the talking. My kids respond better if I listen first. What did your parents do with you?" I asked.

"Nothing!" said Kate, a casually dressed woman sitting beside Stephanie.

"What do you mean?" I asked.

"We never talked about it. My parents are in their late 60's. It wasn't part of their world."

I laughed a little this time myself. My parents are in their 60's and drugs were definitely part of their world.

"What'd you do?" I asked.

Kate looked down a second.

"I didn't really know what to do," she said. "The first time somebody handed me a beer I just walked around with it. I think I took two sips maybe. I have a brother, though. He's really struggling. Alcohol and painkillers, too." She blushed.

"I guess now's a good time to ask if we can keep what's said here within these four walls. Is everyone willing to promise?" Heads nodded as everyone looked around. "I really appreciate it," I added. "Obviously, I can't swear that nobody will say a word, but I promise I'll never identify any of you or your kids. I won't even tell someone you came to this seminar. It's the only way I can get people to really participate, but more than that, I just want to respect your privacy." People looked pleased. "So what else did your parents do?"

"I got a big lecture," said Christine, the dark-haired woman sitting beside Ricardo. "It was one giant sex, boys, drugs, drinking, driving talk. It felt like it went on for about five hours. Then we never discussed it again."

"Yes!" Sebastian said. "I had the same deal, with the threat of an ass-whipping mixed in." Everyone smiled and nodded. Sebastian rubbed his eyes.

"Did it work?" I asked.

"He said, 'If I catch you I'll break your head.'" Sebastian made a fist. "So, I made sure he never caught me!"

Denise, a red-haired young woman who had been taking notes, put down her pen and raised her hand. "My dad's basically an alcoholic. He gets drunk every night. He always said, 'I don't know what to tell you, Honey. Don't turn out like me!'"

"Do other people have parents who use drugs?" I asked.

Bev raised her hand. "My parents are Jamaican. They get high every day. They just said make sure it's not a problem. Get your work done first."

"How's that working out?" I asked.

"It's fine for them. They're still working. I don't really like marijuana," she said. "I get paranoid. I don't want to tell my sons about it, though. My two brothers are complete stoners. They're younger. They have jobs and everything but I think they spend too much time high."

"Nobody has to fess up yet," I said. "But you're not going to surprise me if I learn you've had your first puff."

"Like 100 million other Americans," added Ricardo as he folded his arms.

HOW WE SOUND

"Okay," I started. "I'll be your teen and you all be my parents. I'll say something and you respond."

"Don't forget to roll your eyes when you say it," added Stephanie.

"Will do!" I said. "So here I go. I'm your teen. 'Some cop came to school today. He told a bunch of lies to get us to not smoke pot.'"

"They're trying to talk some sense into you!" said Sebastian loudly.

"If you'd pay attention, you'd see he wasn't lying," said Ada.

"All you kids think you know everything, but you could learn a thing or two if you listened!" said Ricardo.

"You want to end up like your grandpa, drunk every night?" asked Denise.

"Wow!" I said. "So I'm your teen. What do you think I'd say to those responses?" Everyone was silent for a minute.

"That would end the conversation with my boys," Alex said.

"My daughter would probably burst into tears and run to her room," said Kate.

"Why?" I asked.

"That's what she does when I say anything!"

"No kidding!" said Ricardo.

"Can I tell you how I felt?" I asked.

"Go ahead," said Stephanie.

"Pretty sad. I know you were all exaggerating for the role play, but nobody asked me any questions. Everyone was quick to tell me to do something different. Everyone was quick to tell me I am wrong. Of course, as a teen, I see that as a message that I should BE different. And then in my mind that means I'm not good enough the way I am."

"And that must mean we don't love you," Stephanie added.

"Hold on!" said Alex. "I can't handle this thin-skinned stuff. Why is it that every time I tell my son to do something it's got to turn into this whole psychological deal? When I say he should take out the garbage, I'm not talking about who he is as a person."

"You get tired of being misinterpreted. Is that it?" I asked. The parents thought for a moment.

"That's just the way they are," said Christine. "Everything's about who they are as a person."

"Pretty much," said Ricardo.

"Well, I don't know how I can look for these opportunities to talk about drugs," said Alex. "I can't even get him to talk."

"It's hard to get them to open up," I said.

"They don't say anything for weeks and then they spill out in a rage or some kind of weeping bonanza," said Sebastian.

"They're quiet or they freak out," I said. "How am I getting you guys to talk?" They were silent again for a minute.

"You keep asking questions," said Stephanie.

"I keep asking questions," I repeated.

"And you do that therapist thing," she smiled. "You say what we say back to us."

"Yes. That repeating thing. Knock that off!" said Sebastian with a smile. "Tell us what to do!"

"So I'm asking questions and repeating what you say," I said.

"There you go again!" said Sebastian.

"Do you feel like I'm getting to know you?"

"Sort of," said Stephanie.

"Sebastian, Alex, Ricardo—do you guys think I'm getting to know you?"

"Sort of," agreed Ricardo. "I mean, for just being here a couple of minutes."

IT'S ABOUT MORE THAN DRUGS

"Are you saying ask them questions about drugs?" asked Ada.

"It doesn't have to be about drugs," I said. "And I'm not saying you have to grill them when they first walk in the door."

"They hate that," said Denise.

"But what would happen if you nodded your head and let them talk? What would happen if you summarized what they said so they knew you understood them? You know, before you jumped in and told them what to do and how to feel and what to think?" I smiled.

"I'll get bowled over with 900 stories about who wore what outfit at school!" said Kate.

"That's a start," I said. "How do you think they'd feel?"

"Like we're listening," said Elise, a thin woman to my left who hadn't spoken yet. "Like we care."

"Husbands," I added with a smile. "I'm not saying these same questions and summaries will help you get lucky with your wives, but...," I trailed off and the men laughed. The women smiled, too.

"Now that you mention it, I wouldn't mind if someone listened to me a bit myself," said Kate.

"If the kids are home talking to us, at least they're not out with some pusher," said Bev.

"So ask them questions. Say what they said when I get the chance. Ask them about drugs when it comes up. That's it?" asked Ada.

"That's a start," I said. "If you're going to ask them questions, the questions can't be loaded."

"What do you mean?" asked Alex.

"Are your stupid friends still messing up in school?" I said as an example.

"I get you," said Alex.

"Let's do a few of those," I said. "It's fun. Ask me all the questions that really aren't questions at all. Ask me the ones that really just state your opinions and don't show any concern with the answer."

"Are you coming home on time for once?" asked Stephanie.

"Is your homework done?" asked Elise.

"Did you miss the bus, AGAIN?" asked Ricardo.

"What do you need money for this time?" asked Kate.

"Are we going to do this forever?" asked Ada.

"Is that pot I smell?" asked Bev.

"You still beating your wife?" asked Sebastian with a laugh.

"Now you're getting it," I said. "What do you notice?"

"These aren't really questions," said Stephanie. "They're accusations."

"Pretty much," I said. "How is anyone going to feel after these?"

"Accused!" said Ricardo.

"I get your point," said Ada. "We should really listen and ask real questions."

"If you're game, I'd like to have you ask real questions now," I said.

"Okay," said Ricardo.

"So let's go back to the one we did before. I come in and say, 'Some cop came to school today. He told a bunch of lies to get us to not smoke pot.'"

"What makes you think they were lies?" asked Alex.

I stopped and held my hand up.

"How was Alex's question?" I asked.

"It wasn't one," said Sebastian. "He's really saying, 'The policeman didn't lie.'"

"And you're an idiot for thinking so," added Kate.

"You follow?" I asked Alex. He nodded.

"I don't really like this. I just want to tell them and get it over with," Alex said.

"I know what you mean," I said. "It takes longer to listen."

"You're getting to know them, though," said Bev. "You're getting to see how they see the world."

"You get their perspective," I said. "So ask me some more questions. I say: 'A cop came and lied to us about pot.'"

"What did he say?" asked Bev.

"What did you think?" asked Elise.

"How did you feel?" asked Stephanie.

"Now you've got it," I said. "I really like your tone, too. It's hard to explain. You know how someone can ask you a question and use the right words and still make it sound bad?"

"Like 'What did YOU think?'" said Ricardo, with a mocking tone added to the "YOU." "As if what YOU think doesn't really matter."

"That's it," I said. I looked at Alex.

"I get you," he said. "I understand."

"It's not what you say, it's how you say it," said Kate. She was absolutely right.

CHAPTER 2: CREATIVE LISTENING

"Great," I said. "Let's follow up on Kate's comment. She said, 'It's not what you say, it's how you say it.' I think that's a big truth with a capital T." Stephanie smiled at Kate. "The non-verbals, like your body posture and your eye contact, those really make a difference. You can't have a meaningful talk and read the paper at the same time."

"It's as simple as turning your head," Stephanie said.

"Sure," I said. "Imagine this." I looked into my open palm as if I were reading a book, then waved without looking up and said "Love you, honey!" They laughed.

"Obviously, you don't love us enough to look up," Stephanie said.

"Exactly. Do you get that?" Everyone nodded. "Keep an eye out for it. I know you're busy. You can't do a three-hour heart-to-heart every night. But see if you can catch yourself trying to listen to your kids and doing something else at the same time. I'm not saying you've got to hang on their every word, but when they're really serious..."

"Sometimes you're just busy and you probably don't realize you're doing it," said Sebastian.

"I know exactly what you mean," I said.

"Sometimes you don't realize that they're serious right away," said Alex. "They kind of start out slow and then drop a bomb on you."

"I hear you. Once you realize they've got something big on their minds, it can feel nice and dramatic if you suddenly turn off the radio or the TV and look right at them," I said.

"Absolutely," said Ricardo.

"I saw some dad on a cartoon do that," said Kate. "He turned off a baseball game and told his daughter she had his undivided attention. It sounded pretty cool."

"If you're all game, I'd like to go through some other ways to show you're

listening. You can do it without even asking a question. What could you do?"
I asked.

"You can just nod and look them in the eye," Elise said.

"You can say 'Yes' or 'Uh huh' or something," Sebastian added.

"You can do that repeating thing, like you were doing with us," Ada said.

"Exactly," I said. "You all really know this stuff. Now let's do the same drill as before. I come in and say, 'Some cop lied to us about pot.' What do you do?" I looked at Elise. She nodded her head deliberately and raised her eyebrows a little.

"Does everybody see that?" I asked. They all nodded.

"I like the little eyebrow raise," said Kate. "It's kind of a question in itself."

"Good, you're doing it, too," I said to Kate. I looked around and everyone was nodding and raising an eyebrow. It was funny. "Now I assume you all know how to say 'Yes.'"

"Yes," they said.

"There you go! Now what about the reflecting? What about calling it back the way I was doing? How would you do that?" I asked.

"What do you mean?" asked Ricardo.

"I come in and say, 'Some cop lied to us about pot to get us to never smoke it.' What can you say to make it clear that you've heard me?"

"I hear you," said Stephanie.

"Nothing wrong with that," I said. "Think that'll work?"

"I can't just keep saying 'I hear you' over and over," Alex said.

"Luckily, there's more you can do," I said. "There are at least three ways to reflect their words back to them. It's a great way to let them know you understand. First you can just use the same words they say. Everybody with me?" I asked.

"Everybody's with you," said Stephanie with a smile. She was doing exactly what I'd asked.

"Now you've got it!" I said. "You see how she uses my exact words? She just makes it into a statement."

"What do you mean?" asked Ricardo again.

"I said 'Everybody with me?' with my voice going up at the end, to let you know it's a question. Know what I mean?" I asked, with the pitch of my voice going up like a question.

"Yes," Ricardo said. "I know what a question sounds like. In Spanish, you don't even use different words, you just raise your voice like that at the end of what you're saying."

"Great," I said. "But when Stephanie calls it back to me, she says it like a regular statement. She says, 'Everybody's with you.' Her voice stays low at the end of the sentence. So it doesn't sound like a question."

"I hear you," Ricardo said.

"So what?" asked Alex. "What's the big deal?"

"Let me see if I can show you," I said. "Let's get back to the example of your teen coming home. I'm your teen. Reflect back to me. If I say 'A cop lied to us about pot,' what would you say?"

"A cop lied to you about pot," said Ricardo, factually. His voice stayed low at the end of the sentence instead of rising like a question.

"That's it!" I said. "That's exactly." Everyone smiled. "Notice how he makes it a statement." They nodded. "If he made it sound like a question, it's as if he doesn't believe me. You know, it's like 'A cop lied to you?' as if that's just impossible." I raised the pitch of my voice at the end of the question.

"It almost sounds sarcastic," Kate said.

"I see what you mean," said Elise. "It's accusing them again. The question sounds like you don't believe them when they say that the policeman lied."

"Okay," I said. "Everybody get it?"

"I see how to do it," said Alex. "I still don't see why."

"Oh! Can anybody explain?" I asked.

"I think so," said Stephanie. "If you just say their own words like it's a matter of fact, they understand that you heard them without getting defensive and shutting up."

"You've got it," I said, looking at Alex. "It's true. Say what they said as a statement and they'll keep talking. I promise."

"Okay," Alex said. "That's one way."

"You can also paraphrase them. Say what they said but in different words."

"Just use another way of saying the same thing," Stephanie said.

"Exactly," I said.

"No," she laughed. "I'm doing it. I'm saying what you said in different words."

"Oh! You sure did." I laughed, too. "So now let's do it with the cop example. I say 'A cop lied to us about marijuana to get us to stay away from it.' What do you say?"

"A policeman talked to you about drugs at school," said Elise.

"You've got it," I said. "How else could you say it?"

"Today at school a police officer told you about drugs," said Sebastian.

"Yes," I said.

"It seems like a trick," said Alex. "It seems kind of dishonest."

"You don't like the sound of it," I said.

"I can't put my finger on it. It just sounds phony," Alex continued.

"He just did it to you," said Stephanie.

"What?" Alex asked.

"I reflected what you said and you kept talking," I said.

"Oh! I guess so." Alex touched his chin.

"See what I mean?" I asked.

"It sounds natural when you do it," Alex said.

"It does take a little practice," I said. "Just give it some time. If you really hate it, start out slow. Stick with the nods and just saying 'YES.' But let them know you're listening. You'll be amazed. I promise."

"Give it a try," Elise said to Alex.

"So we can say exactly what they said or use different words. Is that all?" asked Ada.

REFLECTING FEELINGS

"There's one more technique you might like. It's called reflecting feelings," I said.

"Oh brother," said Ricardo. Christine grinned.

"You know how it is. Sometimes what they're saying seems to have an emotion behind it. You just give them the name for it," I said.

"I don't want to wind my kids up," said Kate. "They're emotional enough. I don't want to make them angrier than they already are."

"I see what you mean," I said. "But this won't do that, really."

"You don't know my kids," Kate said.

"You can stick to the soft emotions," I added. "The ones that aren't too extreme. Disappointed. Sad. Afraid. Anxious. Worried. That sort of thing."

"What do you mean by 'soft emotions?'" asked Alex.

"They're negative feelings, but they're harder to express. We're good at getting angry and stomping around. The hard, forceful, fighting feelings, those are an American tradition," I said.

"I follow you," said Ricardo.

"The soft emotions are the sadder ones. The ones that might make us vulnerable."

"The soft emotions show your soft side," Stephanie said.

"That's a good way to put it!"

"I can't tell my daughters that they sound mad," said Kate. "Then they really get mad."

"No need to tell them how they sound or what they feel. I hate that myself. You can just say 'sounds disappointing,' or 'how upsetting,' or 'what a drag.' A lot of times, there's a soft emotion underneath all that rage. I know that when I'm mad it's often because I'm hurt, or disappointed, or afraid. Know what I mean?"

"I think so," Kate said.

"I'm not really good at that stuff," Sebastian said.

"Join the club," Ricardo said.

"I know that there are labels on men about this. The stereotype is that men don't know feelings," I said. "But you know sad, glad, afraid, surprised and disgusted."

"They know the words," Stephanie joked.

"At least a couple of them," Christine added.

"Come on, guys, let's show her," I said. "I'll be the teenager again and you reflect my feelings. Show these nice women we know more feelings than horny and angry." Stephanie and Ricardo both chuckled. "Okay, the same drill. 'A cop came to school and told us some lies about pot to keep us away from it.'"

"Sounds disappointing," said Ricardo.

"HURRAY!" I said.

"Congratulations," said Stephanie, clapping softly.

"I don't want to go to all this trouble," said Alex.

"It's more trouble than you want to bother with," I reflected.

"I just don't have the energy to try to figure out what they're feeling. Half the time they don't even know." Alex folded his arms.

"You can always stick to a nod and a 'YES,'" I said. "Even if you guess the wrong feeling, they'll tell you."

"Will they ever!" said Kate.

"Seriously, if you say, 'Sounds disappointing,' and they say, 'Actually, I was mad,' what's the big deal?"

ACCEPTING FEELINGS

"I really don't want them to dwell on things if they're feeling bad," said Elise. "I think it just makes them feel worse."

"What do you all think?" I asked.

"I don't want to see my kids mope around for days," said Stephanie. "But I want them to be able to tell me if they're sad."

"Can you tell us more about that?" I asked.

"In a lot of families," she hesitated and glanced around. "With my parents anyway, we were never allowed to feel bad. We always had to put on a happy face." She smiled a big, phony smile. "It took so much energy. I hated pretending to be happy when I wasn't."

"Anybody else?" I asked.

"We sort of did that, too," said Ricardo. "I think that I would end up being bummed out a lot longer because we were never allowed to talk about it. We weren't even allowed to look sad sometimes."

"It takes a lot of energy to hold back bad feelings," I said. Everyone was quiet. "If you're not allowed to be sad or angry or hurt, well, then how can you be really ecstatic?"

"Yeah!" Sebastian said.

"I know in my family, it sent a strange message," I said. "It's like a parent saying 'Stop feeling bad because you're making me feel bad!' Maybe if our parents could have tolerated bad feelings better, we would have learned to tolerate them, too."

"I hate it when they're sad," said Denise. "I hate it when they feel bad in any way."

"Me, too," I said. "I don't want my girls to ever feel anything bad."

"So there you go!" said Denise.

"How realistic is that?" I asked. "How likely is it that my daughters will never feel bad?"

"Not very!" said Kate.

"I think it's worse in my head than in it is in their hearts." I looked at Denise. "I think I make a bigger deal out of their bad feelings than they do."

"Sometimes," Denise said. "Yes, I guess so."

"I think it's like Ricardo was saying. If you get to really feel it, it sort of runs its course."

"Yes," Ricardo said. "But if you only get to feel it in little bits, it's like it never ends." He shook his head. "It's hard to describe."

"So we can let them see that we're okay with all their emotions. Then they'll become okay with all their emotions, too," I said.

"How do we do that?" asked Denise.

"If we don't rush them through their feelings, if we actually acknowledge that they feel bad, that'll be a great first step," I said.

"I don't think I understand," said Denise.

"Okay," I said, walking closer to her seat. "Imagine I'm your teen. I look really sad and say that I didn't get a part in the school play. What do you say?"

"Don't worry about it!" Denise responded.

"But that's just it," said Stephanie. "That's the problem."

"What could you say instead?" I asked. "What could you say that acknowledged I was sad?"

"I'm sorry, honey," Denise began, "that's a disappointment."

"Exactly!" I said.

"But you're just going to get all weepy now. That's going to make you more sad," Denise added.

"Probably so," I said. "But for how long? How long will I really be sad if you actually acknowledge that I am sad?"

"My kids will mope around for days," she said.

"I think that's when we DON'T acknowledge their feelings," I said.

"That's how it was for me," said Ricardo.

"I think it lasts a long time when you're trying to NOT feel it," I said. "When my girls were babies, if they hurt a finger or something, they'd cry immediately, really loud and really hard, but then it would be over. Know what I mean?"

"Sure," Denise said. "My kids did that."

"I think they got over it because they really felt it. Babies don't know they're not supposed to cry. So they cry with a vengeance. They cry full force. And then when they're done feeling it, they're really done," I said.

"Sad is one thing," Kate said. "But when they're mad, it's different. I don't want them stomping around and breaking things."

"That's completely different," I said. "You don't need to put up with that."

"What do you mean?"

"They can feel however they feel, but that's no excuse for bad behavior," I said. "There's no need to hit people or break stuff."

"That's what they do!" Kate said.

"And what do you do?"

"Punish them."

"Fine with me," I said. "I bet that keeps some of it in check."

"Not as much as I'd like."

"I bet once they get to say that they're mad and really express it, they won't need to stomp around," Stephanie added. Kate nodded.

"I thought we were going to talk about drugs," said Alex.

"Like the acid freaks say," I said, holding my hands together in front of me, "it's all connected."

"Stuffing down bad feelings is what got some of us to abuse drugs in the first place," said Stephanie. "I mean, hypothetically!"

"And once you get into the feelings, I think you're going to have more impact," I said.

"What do you mean?" asked Ricardo.

"In truth, I don't think anybody makes decisions for reasons. You know, we sort of make up logical reasons after the fact. I think it's about feelings. Nobody stays away from drug problems for some technical reason. It's their emotions about it."

"I agree," Sebastian said.

"If we can get them talking about their feelings about anything, anything at all, it'll be easier to get them to talk about their feelings about drugs," I said.

"You think that's better than just warning them?" asked Ada.

"I do," I said. "Let me explain. Didn't your parents and your teachers warn you?"

"Don't get me started with what our teachers used to say," Ricardo added.

"Ha! No kidding," said Alex.

"That sounds like a good place to start," I said. "What's going on in the schools? What about the programs they have in this area?"

CHAPTER 3: JUST SAY NO TO DARE

"Please," said Stephanie, "no government propaganda. We don't want to hear all the lies we got in the DARE program."

"Some of us are too old to know about that stuff," said Ada.

"What happened in DARE?" I asked. Nobody said a word. "Come on! Did they send in a cop to tell you all to 'Just Say No'?"

"Pretty much," said Stephanie.

"We had a policeman come in with all these drugs in a big case," said Bev. "It just made me curious, to tell the truth."

"We used to joke about stealing the drugs," Sebastian said.

"The data are on your side, Bev," I said. "At least one study of DARE showed that it made upper-class kids more likely to experiment with drugs.' What else did they do in DARE?"

"You know," said Alex. "Didn't you have it?"

"No," I said. "I'm too old. When I was in grade school we had these self-esteem programs. Back then, everybody thought that kids did drugs because they had low self-esteem. We sat around talking about how great we were."

"Sounds very educational," Kate said, rolling her eyes.

"In second grade we made these little buttons that said 'ME' that were supposed to show how we were glad to be ourselves."

"There's a nice use of time," Stephanie added.

"I thought so, too," I said. "So I put periods in between the letters and made it my initials. M.E. Mitch Earleywine."

"Glad you got so much out of it," Kate added, shaking her head.

"Did it work?" asked Sebastian.

"I'm afraid not," I said. "We all thought we were so great that we were invulnerable to drugs. At least one study found the same thing.[2] The higher-self-esteem kids end up trying drugs because they think that they're invincible." Everybody was quiet.

"Was that your only drug program?" Bev asked.

"When I was in junior high, we had an alcoholic come talk to us and tell us not to drink."

"We had that!" said Ada.

"Great. So you talk to a police officer who has never done drugs or somebody who can't handle them. How'd that work for you all?" I asked.

Silence.

"It didn't really do much," Christine said.

"Well, the data on DARE are pretty discouraging," I said. "Those who've had it and those who haven't are equally likely to try drugs."[3]

"My parents loved it," said Alex. "My whole school went ape over the thing. We had posters and bumper stickers and workbooks."

"I know that my little ones talk about it like it's good," said Ricardo.

"It was a good idea in the beginning," I said. "You were supposed to have a cool teenager come in and tell you about drugs. The police-officer idea took on a life of its own."

"Didn't it do any good?" asked Ricardo. "We spent so much time."

"Like I said, the research shows that students who had the program are just as likely to use drugs as the students who didn't. There was one positive effect, though."

"What was it?" asked Elise.

"Students who had DARE liked police officers more."[4]

"Come on!" said Alex. "Is this just your interpretation or is this the truth?"

"This isn't just my leftie, pinko propaganda." I smiled at Alex. "The surgeon general declared DARE ineffective. The National Academy of Sciences said it doesn't work. The Department of Education said DARE has been unsuccessful. Those are hardly a bunch of legalizers."

"Then why do we keep doing it?" asked Elise.

"It's popular with a lot of communities. Like Alex said, the police love it. Parents love it. It makes people feel like they're doing something."

"They revamped it," said Ada. "My kids have some new program."

"They have made some changes," I said. "But I'm not optimistic about it. Instead of 'Just Say No,' now they say, 'Use your refusal skills.' I'm not sure that's going to make much of a difference. Why do parents love these programs that focus on peer pressure?"

"It makes your kids look good," said Sebastian. "It makes it look like everything would be fine if it weren't for those bad kids."

"Yes," said Ricardo. "Your own kids are angels who need to resist the neighborhood devil children." He looked around. "You know, if my kids could just stay away from all your kids." He smiled and pointed. I laughed.

"Is that how it works? Are neighborhood devil children holding your kids down and blowing marijuana smoke in their faces?"

"It doesn't really work like that," said Alex. "Your friends are having fun with it and you want to have fun, too."

"Right," said Christine. "It's not that people don't know how to say 'No.' Some people didn't want to say 'No.'"

"The truth comes out," Ricardo said. The two men nodded to each other.

"We used to joke about it," Stephanie added. "If people were getting high and somebody didn't want any, we'd say, 'What's the matter, Mommy won't let you?', like in the role plays. But nobody ever really cared. If somebody didn't want any, that was just more pot for the rest."

"How many of you tried heroin?" I asked. Nobody raised a hand and everyone looked shocked. "You don't really have to answer," I added. "Why didn't more people try heroin?"

"It's skuzzy," said Ricardo. "It's really dangerous."

"What if I were talking to your kids. If I could convince them that marijuana was really dangerous for teens, do you think they would lay off?" There was a long pause. "What do you think?"

"You guys already blew it," said Stephanie. "I mean, not you personally, but all you psychologists. No offense, but you already lied to us. Why should my kids believe you now? I mean...," she trailed off.

"I don't take any offense. No worries," I said. "Believe me, I didn't write the drug programs your kids get in school. But what do you mean?"

"We heard all the lies about pot. It's hard to trust anything else we hear. I can't expect my kids to listen to the same bull," said Alex.

"Next time," I said, looking at my watch, "we'll clear up all the lies about marijuana. We need to call it a night." I was pleased with how everything was going, and realized I wasn't nervous anymore. "I appreciate everybody jumping in," I said. "It's obvious that you all really care. Let's do a little summary so I don't forget everything we said."

"You do it," said Ada.

"I'll go first. We talked about finding opportune times to discuss drugs without turning it into a lecture." I wrote "OPPORTUNITIES" on the board. "Then what?" I asked.

"Saying 'Yes' and nodding to let them know we're listening," said

Alex.

"Great!" I said. I wrote "LISTENING" on the board. "What else?"

"Saying their own words back to them so they know we're listening," said Ricardo.

"Yes, the reflecting," I said. I wrote "REFLECTIONS" on the board.

"Giving them feeling words for what they're saying," said Stephanie.

"Good," I said. I wrote "REFLECT FEELINGS."

"Letting them have bad feelings in the first place," said Kate.

"Accepting their feelings," I said, and wrote "ACCEPTANCE." "And last but not least?"

"Don't count on DARE to do our job," said Denise.

"Great. I would write DARE with a line through it, but I don't want to get us all busted." They laughed.

"We didn't talk much about marijuana," said Alex.

"I wish we had covered everything," I said. "If you do all this stuff, though, I think you'll see some good changes at home. Give it a shot and let me know how it goes. I'll see you next time." I waved as people headed for the door.

Ada came up to me as I was getting my coat. "I still don't know what to tell my kids!"

"How old are they?"

"They're 11 and 8. They're good boys. I just don't want them to get involved with all of this."

"Do you think they're getting high now?"

"Oh no!" she said. "But it's around. It's in the neighborhood. Their uncles get high, too."

"We'll get into it. For now, there's no need to give them a big lecture. Just listen to them. Tell them you love them. Let them know why it's important to be healthy."

"I do that anyway," she said.

"Then you're on the right track. Don't worry. We'll talk about it all next time."

"Well, thanks!" Ada smiled and waved. Alex came up behind her.

"I kind of want to talk to you about something. I kind of don't. What if we're still getting high sometimes? I mean, not like an addict or anything, but once in awhile."

"We'll cover that next time, too," I said. "But the truth is obvious. It's up to you. I think that you know your kids better than I do. I know plenty of parents who don't tell their kids all of their personal business. This might fall into that category."

"I see what you mean," he said, and waved as he walked out.

I looked forward to our next meeting the whole week. I'm always eager to see how many people show for the second session, because they're the ones who usually stay for the whole series. I found myself thinking a lot about what we said about bad feelings. A paper of mine had been rejected from a good scientific journal. This happens all the time, but for some reason this one had hit me hard. I had written a paper that criticized the work on marijuana and mental illness. I felt that the journal editor was really picky. I wondered if he would have been so picky if my work had said that marijuana made everyone insane.

The odd thing was that I had tried to keep myself from feeling bad about it. I had just spent all this time talking to parents about letting their kids feel bad, and here I was not allowing myself to feel bad. I went to my office and shut the door and gave it some thought. Then I felt really angry with the editor, and the field of psychology, and the world. Then I felt sad. I called my wife and talked about it. After awhile I was surprised at how sad I felt about it. Then it all seemed a little stupid. It was just a paper. Big deal. I decided I would make some changes and send it to another journal. I felt a lot better. Then I thought the whole incident would make a good story to tell the parents if I could fit it into the conversation. I felt good about that idea.

I reached the room and many people had already arrived. They were chatting happily.

"The same thing happened with my daughter," said Kate.

"I was surprised," said Stephanie.

"What happened?" I asked, taking off my jacket.

"We were just saying that the chance to talk about drugs came up more often than we expected," Stephanie said.

"It's all over the TV," said Kate. More people entered the room and greeted us with a nod or a wave.

"So, did you ask your kids about it?" I asked.

"They've got a lot more going on than I thought," said Stephanie.

"Even my 10-year-old had stuff to say about cigarettes," said Ricardo. "But you've got to let them talk."

"I agree," I said. Many people nodded. "Any success stories?" Everyone hesitated at first.

"I did end up talking about meth with my older one. There was a special on the news that really made it sound disgusting," Kate said. "I would've jumped right in with a big lecture, but I just asked her if she'd heard of it. At first I got a lot of one-word answers, but I just kept saying things back to her, like you said. By the end she was promising me she would never do it, telling me not to worry, and all that."

"Did you believe her?" I asked.

"Yes. It's kind of hard to explain. It seemed like she really did think it was bad and didn't want me to get upset. It was actually kind of sweet," Kate said.

"I didn't talk about drugs, but I had a good talk with my son," Alex said.

"How'd it go?" I asked.

"He got in a fight after school. I was busy and I started out saying that he knows better—all the stuff that we were saying that we hated about our own parents. But I stopped and asked what happened and actually listened. Man, I got an earful. I didn't jump in until he was done. I didn't do that feeling thing that you do, but I definitely nodded and said 'yes' a lot," Alex said.

"Great," I said. "What happened?"

"It turns out it was just this misunderstanding with one of our neighbors. I didn't even tell him what to do. He got on the phone and they worked it out themselves. It probably didn't take any longer than if I had lectured him and told him what to do. I was very pleased. He's turning into a good little man," Alex said.

"Did you tell him that?" Stephanie asked.

"I will when I get home," Alex answered.

"That's great, Alex," I said. "Stephanie's point is a good one, too. They need all the praise we can offer. It's not as if they have their own personal cheerleaders following them around to rant and rave every time they do something right."

"I wouldn't mind one of those myself," said Elise.

"I don't think my wife would like the idea of my own little cheerleader," said Sebastian with a grin.

"In the spirit of dishing out the praise," I said, "thanks for making it here again. I know you're all busy. Any other success stories about letting your kids feel their feelings or talking about drugs?"

"Yes," said Elise. "My daughter got dumped by her boyfriend. I don't really like the guy and I almost said so. But instead I told her how sad I was one time when I got dumped. I was going to wrap it up with how I found someone else, but I just left it at the sad part. She cried. I was worried that I had made it worse. But it only took a couple of minutes, like Ricardo said. She wasn't dancing around or anything, but she didn't look as sad as when I first came in."

"This is interesting," I said. "I never thought about how letting them have their feelings actually saves time. I guess it does. You folks must be

really busy." Everyone nodded. "Then let me thank you all again," I
added.

CHAPTER 4: MARIJUANA MISINFORMATION

"We're very busy," said Alex. "So let's talk about grass this time."

"Marijuana it is," I said. "You mentioned last time that the psychologists had all lied to you. We had lost credibility. Let's clear this up. What did you hear about marijuana? Let's separate the truth from the lies," I said. "This will help you make sure you're telling your kids the truth. You'll blow their minds if you know this. I mean it. Go ahead, call it out! What did you hear?"

"Marijuana will make you stick a needle in your arm!" said Stephanie. I went to the board behind me and wrote "GATEWAY."

"You'll get hooked," said Bev. I wrote "DEPENDENCE."

"Marijuana will make you violent," said Sebastian. I wrote "AGGRES-SION" on the board.

"Yeah," added Ricardo. "It'll make you accidentally shoot your best friend with your dad's pistol." People grinned. "You've seen the commercial."

"The new pot is super strong," said Sebastian. I wrote "POTENCY" on the board.

"It makes you not want to do anything," said Ada. I wrote "AMOTIVA-TION."

"You'll run over a kid on a bike at the drive-through, like in that other commercial," said Bev. Everyone grinned again. I wrote "DRIVING" on the board.

"What about lung cancer?" Stephanie asked. I wrote "CANCER" on the board.

"It'll make you crazy," said Denise, twirling her finger beside her head to make the "loony" gesture. I wrote "MENTAL ILLNESS."

"It kills brain cells," said Alex. I wrote "THE BRAIN" on the board.

"Wow!" I said. "You folks sure heard a lot about marijuana. Let me walk through these in order. Most of what you heard was exaggerated or out-right wrong. That doesn't mean that marijuana is some kind of vitamin pill. It doesn't even mean that it's safe for teens."

"That's no reason to lie to us," Stephanie said.

"I agree. I promise that I'm not going to lie to you. Okay?" A few folks nodded. "I don't think that the drug czar or your parents or your teachers meant to lie. They're just scared. Nobody wants to see kids end up with a drug problem. They were doing the best that they could. But you'll do better for your kids."

"Yeah, yeah. We heard that," said Stephanie.

"Let's cover as much as we can," I said.

GATEWAYS AND STEPPING STONES

"Let's start with the gateway theory. The idea was that marijuana leads to harder drugs. How was this supposed to work?" I asked.

"They never really explained," said Ricardo. "One day you were smoking a joint and the next day you were in the gutter."

"We heard that you get bored," said Bev. "You'd use pot for awhile and get tired of it, so you were supposed to use cocaine. Then you were supposed to get tired of that. And so on."

"Did you believe it?" I asked. No one raised a hand. "Why not?"

"It doesn't make any sense! We knew people who got high and didn't do other drugs," said Sebastian.

"They told us that every heroin addict started with pot," said Elise. "Isn't that what a gateway is?"

"I guess that's the issue," I said. "What is a gateway anyway?" No one answered. I waited. Still no response. "I think the confusion comes from the definition of 'gateway.' When I was in school they called this 'The Stepping Stone Theory.' Somehow, marijuana was supposed to make you crave hard drugs the way salt makes you thirsty. It wasn't just that people tried marijuana first. Marijuana MADE you take hard drugs."

"Yes," said Ada. "They never came right out and said it that way, but that was the message."

"Research doesn't really support the idea that marijuana causes other drug use. First of all, millions of people who try pot never use any other illegal drugs. Most of them don't even use marijuana that much." I went to the board and wrote "MARIJUANA" and drew an arrow to "HARD DRUGS." Then I put a line through the arrow. "About 100 million Americans have tried marijuana, like Ricardo said. But where are all the heroin addicts?" I asked. "Most people who tried marijuana have never even seen heroin. How many of you have ever seen heroin?" Again, no one said a word.

"You asked us that already," Ricardo said.

"Just making a point," I said. "In addition, at least three studies of drug users in treatment show a lot of them do not start with marijuana. They use whatever drug is most available. In crack neighborhoods, people try crack before they try marijuana."[5]

"But what about the order?" asked Ada. "You know, first alcohol, then cigarettes, then pot, then coke, like that."

"Again," I smiled, "no one needs to fess up about anything." Ada shook her finger at me.

"I'm not talking about myself, mister," she said.

"A lot of people who use hard drugs do follow a progression," I said. "That doesn't mean the first drug caused the use of the next." People still looked confused. "Everybody who rides a motorcycle starts out riding bicycles. That doesn't mean riding a bike causes you to ride a motorcycle."

"I get it," Ada said.

"For what it's worth," I said, "my friend Linda Collins at Penn State showed that kids who drink a lot of caffeine when they're young are the ones who try drugs later.[6] Should we make caffeine illegal?"

"Please no!" blurted Denise, and she took a big swig from her cup of coffee.

"Also," I said, "the drug that really separates folks who go on to hard drugs from the others isn't marijuana. Guess what it is?"

"Alcohol?" asked Kate.

"No," I said. "Almost everybody drinks."

"Cigarettes!" said Sebastian.[7]

"I'm afraid so. Kids who become regular smokers—they are the ones most likely to try other drugs. Think we'll be hearing about cigarettes as a gateway drug anytime soon?"

"Not unless you want another Civil War," said Alex.

"Damn!" said Ada. "I knew those cigarettes were serious."

"It's true in a sense. People who like to do drugs—they like to do drugs. So people who like marijuana often do try hard drugs," I said.

"It's sort of a gateway, though. Marijuana comes first for a lot of people who end up addicted to other drugs. What's the harm in explaining it that way?" Elise asked.

"I have a couple of worries about that," I said. "First off, the idea that marijuana leads to hard drugs can actually create a self-fulfilling prophecy."

"What do you mean?" Ricardo asked.

"If enough people believe that marijuana leads to hard drugs, once they try marijuana, they might go ahead and try hard drugs, too."

"I still don't follow, Mr. Professor," Kate said.

"Yeah, speak English." Ricardo smiled.

"It's related loosely to something called the abstinence violation effect, or what I call the 'What the Hell' effect. My friend Alan Marlatt took a bunch of alcoholics who believed that one drink would send them on a giant, uncontrollable bender. He gave some of them a placebo, a fake drink, but told them it was alcohol. Sure enough, they ended up drinking more later. He gave others alcohol but didn't tell them, and they didn't go into a big drinking fit."[8]

"So it's in their minds!" Ricardo blurted.

"Once they thought that they had one drink, a lot of them said 'What the Hell' and went ahead and drank more. What they expected to happen actually happened. Even if they only thought that they'd had alcohol, it made them drink more later."

"What's that got to do with marijuana as a gateway?" Elise asked.

"I'm afraid that saying marijuana is a gateway gives some people, especially teens, the expectation that it IS a gateway. Once they try marijuana they expect to go on and try cocaine or some other drugs, and then a few of them do," I said.

"What should we tell them instead?" asked Kate.

"Spread the word that lots of people try pot and never use hard drugs," I said. "First of all, it's true. They could learn that even if they've tried marijuana, they don't have to keep using it. And they certainly don't have to try hard drugs. Can you imagine that?"

"Then they wouldn't be afraid of marijuana!" Ada said.

"But if they're afraid of marijuana for a reason that isn't true, what happens when they find out it's a lie?" Everyone was silent. "What happens when they meet people who smoke marijuana but don't do hard drugs?"

"They don't believe you anymore. They think you lied to them about pot so they think you lied about everything," said Sebastian.

"If you lie to them once, it's all over," Ricardo said.

"Exactly," I said. "We lose credibility completely. Then, when I say that methamphetamine shrinks your brain, they won't believe that, either. And it's true."

"Okay, I get you," said Kate.

"One other thing. It's only my clinical impression, but I've heard it enough now to worry. People who believe the gateway story end up using dangerous drugs instead of marijuana. I've had clients tell me that they heard that marijuana led to heroin so they sniffed glue or huffed gas instead. Inhalants are much worse than marijuana. It's just a shame," I said.

"That's gross," said Stephanie.

"So does that cover the gateway theory?" They nodded. "Lots of people who use hard drugs used marijuana first, but that doesn't mean marijuana caused hard-drug use. Plenty of people who use marijuana never use hard drugs, and plenty of people who use hard drugs didn't start with marijuana. Got it?"

"Got it," said Stephanie.

"What do you think your kids will say to this?" I asked.

"I'm not telling them," said Bev. "I mean, if they ask, I'll say what you said."

"It's not exactly an opener," said Alex, leaning forward. "I can't say: 'It's not a gateway, but don't smoke pot!' It just doesn't sound like a good pitch!"

"What about the violence and the fighting?" asked Elise.

"Let's take a break first," I said. "Please be back in five minutes."

MARIJUANA AND AGGRESSION

As people gradually came back from the hall, Ada said, "This class is going better than I expected."

"I think so, too!" I said.

"I thought it was just going to be the usual stuff," said Kate. "You know—watch 'em every minute, take 'em to church, tell 'em it's evil."

"You can do all that if you want," I said. Everyone returned. People brought sodas and seemed more comfortable.

"I really do appreciate how much everyone is jumping in," I said. "Thanks. It makes things easier for me."

I went to the board where I had written "AGGRESSION" in big letters.

"I honestly don't know where to begin with this," I said. "What have you heard?"

"They never came right out and said that marijuana made you angry when I was in school," said Kate. "All the drugs got lumped together and they all made you a crazy criminal."

"I saw it on a Web site," said Ricardo. "One of the government sites said delinquent kids smoke pot."

"Anybody who thinks marijuana causes aggression has obviously never been high," I said. A few parents smiled. "When people get high in the laboratory, they're no more aggressive than the folks who smoke the placebo weed—the fake pot that has no effect."[9] I let that idea sink in for a moment. "In one study, the people who got high were less aggressive than the other folks. It's true even when they're provoked. Marijuana intoxication just doesn't seem to lead to aggression."

"How do they test that?" Sebastian asked. "What do they do, get them stoned and punch them or something?"

"Most of these studies use some form of competition. People play a game against each other. Whoever wins gets to take points away from the other guy or blast him with a loud sound or make him stick his hand in ice water. One of the contestants is the experimenter's stooge. He automatically takes a lot of points away or blasts the participants with a long, loud noise. Then they see what the other people do."

"So the stoned guys don't do anything?" Sebastian asked.

"It's not that. They play the game. They're just not any more aggressive than anybody else."

"Well, then how did this idea that marijuana causes aggression get started?" asked Ada.

"There's an old story and a new story," I said.

"Please don't tell it!" said Stephanie.

"I'll keep it brief. The old story was about the assassins. Anybody know this one?"

"We heard this," said Ricardo. "Some guy in ancient times had all his soldiers eat hashish and then go kill people. Everybody called them the 'hashishans' and that got turned into 'assassins.' Something like that."

"That's pretty much it," I said. "The guy was named Hasan. The year was around 1100. He apparently did have a lot of good fighters working with him. But the story gets a little confused. In one version, he gives them a drug, they pass out, and they wake up in this garden with lots of wonderful things. It's supposed to be like heaven. Then he gives them a drug again, they pass out, and they wake up back at the base camp. He tells them that if they fight hard they'll get to go back to the garden when they die."

"What's that got to do with pot?" asked Bev.

"I really don't know. But the 'assassin' stuff really stuck. The idea that 'assassin' comes from 'hashish' probably isn't true, either." I wrote both words on the board. Then I wrote "HASAN." "The way to say 'follower of Hasan' would be 'Hassassan,'" I said, writing that word, too. So 'assassin' probably just means 'follower of Hasan.' The Arabic word for 'kill' is apparently 'hassass,'" I added, writing this word on the board. "So Hassassan, or assassin, probably just means 'killer.'"

"How'd this catch on?" asked Stephanie.

"Harry Anslinger, America's first drug czar, brought it up to congress in the 1930's. Marijuana was still legal. He was trying to emphasize how dangerous it was, so he told them this old story."

"Marijuana's illegal because of some old legend?" asked Alex.

"Don't get me started," I said.

"What's the new story?" Sebastian asked.

"The new story is based on big surveys. A lot of people who admit to doing hostile stuff also admit to smoking pot."

"That doesn't prove anything!" said Alex.

"It doesn't prove that smoking pot makes you aggressive," I said. "But it does prove that some aggressive people smoke pot."

"Were they even high when they did this hostile stuff?" asked Ada.

"That's the question," I said. "My student Tom Denson and I showed that it's not the case. When you ask people if they did aggressive things, they often say that they did. Not just punching somebody out, but throwing things or calling people names. But if you ask if they were high at the time, they rarely were."[10]

"Is that it?" asked Elise. "That can't be all there is to it."

"There was one study that looked at psychopaths. They were aggressive when they were high. Eight—count them, eight—psychopaths got high and got more aggressive afterward. I'm not sure what to make of that."[11]

"Okay," said Stephanie. "No gateway. No violence. What else?"

"Let me just add one thing, though. When it comes to drugs causing aggression, there's nothing as alarming as alcohol. My laboratory and lots of labs around the country show it. Drunk people like to punch people. Alcohol really does increase aggression. So don't drink too much and stay away from folks who do! If you think it'll help your kids stay away from alcohol, please mention this."[12]

"They know," said Denise. "They've seen their grandfather."

"Oh please," said Ada. "Don't get me started."

"Can we talk about that a minute?" asked Kate. "I mean, it sounds like alcohol is more dangerous than marijuana, really."

"You could make that argument," I said. "Let me get to it after we discuss marijuana and the brain. The impact of alcohol is much worse. You mind waiting?"

"I hate waiting," said Stephanie. "But I'll do it."

"I still feel like I've got no ammunition," said Alex. "If I say that there's no gateway and it doesn't make you aggressive, that doesn't explain why they shouldn't do it."

CHAPTER 5: TALKING ABOUT YOUR OWN USE AND PROBLEMS

Alex certainly had a point. I wanted to dispute all of the myths about marijuana before getting into the real reasons that teens need to stay away from it. But the difficult task of discussing a parent's use reared its head.

"We'll get there," I said. "Let's get the myths out of the way first. I think your kids will be impressed if you don't simply repeat the same stuff they heard at school."

"They're going to wonder how we know," said Bev, looking down.

"Blame it on me!" I said.

"We understand," said Elise, looking at everyone. "But what are we supposed to say when they put the screws to us? They want to know if we tried it."

"Let's talk about it," I said. "What do you think?"

"We can't win," said Sebastian. "If we say we never did it, then they think we don't know anything. If we say we did try it, then they say that they should get to."

"He's right," said Alex. "And if you didn't turn into a complete addict then they use that against you."

"What do you mean?" I asked.

"If we say that we tried it and our lives aren't a total wreck, then they say that they should get to try it, too!"

"Even if you tried it only once, then they're going to argue that they can try it once," Stephanie added.

"But if you lie to them and say you never tried, they don't believe it anyway," said Ricardo.

"Sounds like your kids are pretty smart," I said.

"Just smart enough to get into trouble," said Kate. Everyone was quiet for a minute.

"So what do we say?" asked Elise.

"What have you tried telling them?" I asked.

"Mostly, I just dodge the topic," Alex said.

"Yes," said Sebastian. "Just avoid the issue."

"How's that working out?" I asked.

"You can see," said Stephanie. "We're obviously still worried. I, for one, don't know if I can keep it up."

"It just feels bad," said Alex.

"Whoa!" said Kate with a laugh. "Alex almost had a feeling."

"It's complicated," I began.

"If you say 'it depends,' we're going to throw stuff at you," said Denise.

"I wish I had some magic words that would work every time," I said. "I do have the next best thing." I paused and thought.

"What's that?" asked Alex.

"It really is different with each relationship. I'm sure you can imagine saying one thing to one of your children that you wouldn't say to another."

"Yes, but they talk to each other," said Elise.

"They sure do," said Kate.

"So here's the story. Let's walk through the options and guess what would happen. It's a good way to solve any problem," I said.

"Some parents really have never done it," said Denise. "They could tell the truth."

"Great." I smiled. "And why didn't these hypothetical parents ever try it?"

"It wasn't around as much," said Denise. "I knew my father had alcohol problems and I didn't want to risk it. I just didn't think it was worth trying. It sounds weird, I know, growing up when we did."

"More Americans haven't tried than have," I said.

"Or so they say," Ricardo said with a nod.

"We could lie and say we never did it," said Elise. "We could say the same stuff Denise just said, even if it wasn't technically true."

"What would happen?" I asked.

"They'd catch on eventually. If they believed it in the first place," said Stephanie.

"What do you think, Elise?"

"I never even did it that much," she said. "And I waited until I was in college."

"We could say we did it and it was bad," said Bev. "I didn't like getting all paranoid and nervous."

"Nothing wrong with telling the truth," I said. "If you had a bad reaction they certainly ought to hear about it."

"Does that run in families?" asked Ricardo.

"At least one study suggests it does.[3] If you had a weird reaction, your kids might, too. I was actually thinking about people who had problems," I said.

"My brothers...," said Bev. "I can always point to them."

"If you've got any drug dependence in the family, that seems worth mentioning, but we're drifting from the topic of our own use. It's hard to talk about," I said.

"I'm going to stick with my story that I never tried it. Maybe when they're older I'll fess up. But right now I don't want to get into it," said Elise.

"There are a lot of things they never need to know I did," said Alex.

"If you're comfortable," I said, "that's fine. Do you think they'll believe it?"

"I think so," said Elise.

"I'm actually not so sure, at least for me," said Alex.

"Just give us some suggestions," said Stephanie.

"A friend of mine had an interesting story. He asked his sons if they would believe him if he said he'd never tried," I said.

"If I said I'd never tried, you wouldn't believe me. If I said I did try, you'll use it against me," said Kate. "I think my older girl would get a kick out of that. She might cut me a little slack."

"When I teach people how to do therapy, we call it 'sharing the dilemma,'" I said.

"So you just say that you know you can't win?" asked Ricardo.

"You just said it very well before," said Stephanie to Ricardo.

"She's right!" I agreed. "You know better how your kids would react than I would."

"What if you still use?" asked Alex. "You know, hypothetically, once in awhile."

"Yes, hypothetically," grinned Ricardo.

"My brother tells a story about Gandhi and a kid who ate too much sugar. Anybody know it so I don't have to tell it?"

"I've heard this one," said Stephanie. "A woman wants Gandhi to tell her son to stop eating so many sweets. Gandhi tells her to come back in three days. When they return, Gandhi tells the boy that he shouldn't eat sugar because it's bad for him, so please knock it off. The woman says, 'Why'd we have to wait three days for that?', and Gandhi says, 'I had to stop eating sweets myself.'"

"Ow!" said Kate.

"Come on!" said Alex. "Are you saying parents have to stop if they want their kids to stop? What about alcohol?"

"Here's what I'm saying," I said. "If you get high in front of them, or marijuana's a problem for you, then you've got more of an uphill climb. Would you agree?"

"This is impossible," said Alex.

"Okay," said Ricardo. "I understand not getting high in front of them."

"It seems kind of dishonest," said Denise.

"I don't have sex in front of them," said Ricardo.

"Please!" said Kate.

"Why are you hedging on this one?" Sebastian asked.

"I guess you caught me." I sighed. "The truth is, I like doing these seminars. I love talking to students and I love talking to parents."

"So?" Stephanie asked.

"I honestly can't say that adult marijuana use is a bad thing. But every time I come out about it, I get threats."

"What do you mean?" Kate asked.

"Nobody ever says that I'm not going to get to teach anymore. But I do get lots of concerned advice."

"Nobody wants to see you get in trouble. That's cute!" Elise smiled.

"But I'm not going to lie to you. Adults can use marijuana without developing problems. Literally millions of them do. It happens at least 90 percent of the time."

"So should we tell our kids?" Christine asked.

"It's up to you, obviously. But just like alcohol and chainsaws and driving, I think it's fine for adults and worth explaining that way. I know it's an uphill battle, but it's honest. I can't stand here and tell you to lie to your own kids. I just can't."

"What if you do have a problem, though?" Alex asked.

"Seems like the same deal to me," I said. "What better warning against use can there be than your own problem experience?"

"Seriously, though," said Ricardo. "How do you know who's got a problem?"

"What a coincidence," I said, pointing to the word "DEPENDENCE" on the board. "That's what's next on our list."

DEPENDENCE AND PROBLEMS

"Cheap segue!" Sebastian said.

"Cut me a little slack," I begged. "So how do we know who's got a problem with marijuana?"

"I've seen this get pretty crazy," said Kate. "We had a guy come to the dorm in college and say that any use is abuse."

"Abuse actually has a formal definition," I said. "Simple use isn't enough. There are four symptoms and any one would qualify for abuse."[14]

"Well, what are they?" Ada asked.

"Messing up your obligations, getting high in unsafe settings, legal troubles and using even when you've got problems."

"Sounds kind of subjective," Sebastian said.

"I don't think it's worth nitpicking about," I said.

"Who decides this stuff anyway?" asked Alex.

"Mostly old white men with lots of degrees," I said. "They beat each other up and waste a lot of paper splitting hairs about who's dependent and who isn't."

"Can we skip that part?" asked Stephanie.

"With pleasure," I said. "Let me just give you the bottom line on dependence. There are a bunch of symptoms and you have to have at least three, but the hallmarks are tolerance and withdrawal."

"What do those mean, really?" Stephanie asked.

"In so many words, tolerance means it takes more drugs than it used to for you to get the same buzz. Withdrawal means you feel rotten when the drug is gone."

"Who has marijuana withdrawal?" Sebastian asked.

"That's just it," I said. "It took decades for scientists to find marijuana withdrawal. It's really just nervousness and craving. It's not like our stereotype of kicking heroin or anything."

"What about psychological dependence?" Ada asked.

"In theory, physical dependence has tolerance and withdrawal, any other kind of dependence would focus on the other symptoms."

"What are those?" Christine asked.

"Using more than you meant to, wanting to cut down but you can't, that sort of thing. I think it's stupid, personally. I'd rather focus on problems. The bottom line is if the drug messes up your life."

"Whatever that means," said Ricardo.

"Your social life, your recreation, your work—those would be good places to start," I said.

"Give us some examples," said Ada. "Please."

"Legal trouble is probably the one that gets people most emotional. If I'm working with a marijuana abuser who has been busted, or even when I'm talking about abuse to my class, there's a lot of anger about that one. It's part of the definition of abuse."

"What do you mean?" asked Stephanie.

"It's just that people who use alcohol or legal drugs don't get into legal trouble the same way," said Denise. "You can't get busted just for owning a fifth of vodka, but you can for a bag."

"That's messed up," said Alex.

"The legal problems are really the worst of all for adults," I said. "There were over 700,000 marijuana arrests last year."

"That's a lot of police time," said Ricardo.

"Teens are particularly vulnerable on this one," I said. "They're easy to bust."

"If it keeps them from getting into worse trouble, though...." Bev trailed off.

"I'd just like to think cops have something better to do," said Sebastian.

"I don't think we'll resolve this here," I said. "If you'd like to see these laws change, there are plenty of good people on your side. Check out the National Organization for the Reform of Marijuana Laws. They're at norml.org on the Web. Or see the Marijuana Policy Project's site at mpp.org. Or see the Drug Policy Alliance at drugpolicy.org. There are lots of Americans who are upset about the Drug War."

"Thanks for the public-service announcement," said Kate. "Can we get back to our kids?"

"Truth be told, changing the laws could help your kids in the long run. I think that as far as your kids are concerned, a marijuana bust can be a lot of trouble. Who cares if it should or shouldn't qualify as abuse? It's going to cost you time and money and effort. It's a problem," I said.

"Does that mean you're addicted, though?" asked Alex.

"Addiction is another one of those terms without a formal definition," I said. "I think if your kids are going to school high, they can't learn. If they're missing school or work because they're stoned, that's a problem. If they don't do anything fun without getting high, that's a problem."

"I get the idea," said Stephanie. "If they give up their after-school activities to get high, that's a problem."

"Sure," I said. "If they used to play sports or music or do art or read for fun, but now they just get high.... You get the idea." Everybody was quiet. "It's the same for you. It's the same for us adults."

"What are you saying?" asked Sebastian.

"If we forget to pick them up from soccer practice because we're baked," I said. Then I paused and said, "You guys call out the problems!"

"If we're missing work because we're high," said Stephanie.

"If we get busted, God forbid," said Kate.

"If we're driving them around town high," said Sebastian.

"If we can't help them with homework because we're too high," said Ricardo.

"You got it," I said. "Any interference with parenting would certainly be a problem. Any screwing up at work, too. There's a social and recreational side that I think is easy to ignore, too. I don't mean to sound like anyone's mom."

"Don't worry!" said Ada. "No danger of that."

"If it's your only way to have fun, or it's all you do with your friends, that ought to make you wonder, too."

"I get you," said Alex. "I get you."

"It sounds like you're saying that if it's a problem, it's a problem," Ricardo said.

"I never thought about it like that. I don't mean for it to sound so circular. But yes, if it's keeping you from doing what you need to do, then that's trouble. Should we make a big list?"

"I think we know what you mean," Elise said.

"You really have to be honest with yourself," I said. "I guess that's the most adult part about it."

CHAPTER 6: AMOTIVATION

"What about this laziness, the people who don't want to do anything? Wouldn't that be a problem?" Ada asked.

I pointed to where I had written "MOTIVATION" in big letters on the blackboard. "You've all seen the movies and heard the jokes. Your kids sang along with the Afroman song." I said. A few people grinned.

"What's that?" asked Denise.

"Can someone explain?" I asked.

"This guy had this hit song," started Sebastian. "He talked about all the things he was going to do, but instead he just got high. In the end he says he's messing up the song itself because he's high, and if the record doesn't sell, it's because he's high. That sort of thing."

"Sounds like a laugh riot," Kate said sarcastically.

"It was really popular," said Ricardo.

"The idea that marijuana saps your motivation is popular, too," I said. "Why doesn't that keep kids away?"

"They just don't believe it," Ada said, shaking her head.

"It's become such a stereotype I'm not even sure what to say," I began. "We joke about it a lot and it's come back to bite us. What is amotivational syndrome anyway?"

"That's when you smoke so much pot that you don't want to do anything," Sebastian said.

"The first talk of this lack of motivation started at least a hundred years ago," I said.

"Whoa, really?" asked Kate.

"Yes, this big British study in the late 1800's. The Indian Hemp Drugs Commission couldn't find any problems in adult users. The term 'amotivational' didn't start until the late 1960's. Teens who smoked pot were supposed to be these apathetic slugs who never did anything."

"I've seen it," said Alex. "Everybody knows some stoner who doesn't do much."

"Probably so," I said. "But we forget all the lazy people we know who never smoke pot."

"Hmm," said Denise. "I never thought of that."

"We also forget about all the successful adults who use marijuana. We tend to remember information that fits our stereotypes and forget the rest. I can't give examples without sounding racist or sexist, but we definitely see the world through our prejudices."

"Go ahead and give examples," said Stephanie. "We won't snitch."

"For one, the idea that women can't do math is just a stereotype. People tend to remember women who are bad at math but forget all the women who are good at it. They also forget all the guys who are bad at math."

"No kidding!" said Sebastian.

"Let's just look at the stereotype of marijuana users as lazy. My own work shows that people who get high every day claim to be just as motivated as folks who've never smoked,"[15] I said.

"Those guys are just lying," said Alex. "No offense."

"None taken," I said. "They could be lying. So let's look at data on other measures." I went to the board and wrote "GRADES, EMPLOYMENT, LABORATORY WORK." "In college students, you compare pot smokers to non-smokers. Who has the higher grades?" Everyone was silent. "Neither one," I said. "They're both the same."[16] Everyone stared for just an instant, then nodded. "Actually, two studies showed that the college students who smoked marijuana had higher grades." [17]

"It's no study aid!" Stephanie said.

"That's for sure," Kate said.

"Oh! I didn't mean to give that impression. Nobody learns new material high. But my point is that there's no support for the idea that marijuana saps motivation in college students."

"I'll buy that," Elise said.

"Now the employment data," I said. "Pot smokers and non-smokers. If there really was an amotivational syndrome, who should make less money, take more days off and lose their jobs more often?"

"Smokers," Stephanie said.

"But they don't," I said. "They report the same salaries, the same number of sick days and the same job turnover. In one study, the men who smoked marijuana actually made more money."[18]

"There's a way to get a raise!" Sebastian said.

"I don't think smoking marijuana helped them earn more money," I said. "I think that having more money helped them afford some pot."

"What about in the laboratory?" Kate looked up as she spoke.

"There are really two kinds of laboratory studies. Some of them have people come to the laboratory and get high or smoke a placebo and then do some task. My friend Bob Pihl at McGill University did one. Once people were high, he said that they could get more money if they pushed a button faster when a light went on.[19] You can guess how a high person feels about pushing a button when a light goes on."

"That'll just wreck your buzz," said Bev.

"So during intoxication, people won't do these things, at least in some studies."

"That's hardly some kind of syndrome," said Alex.

"I agree," I said. "Other studies have people work for money in a laboratory for multiple days. They smoke on some days and not on others."

"Where do we sign up?" asked Bev.

"It's hard to get funding for this sort of work anymore," I said. "A lot of these studies were done over 20 years ago."

"So what happened?" asked Kate.

"One study had men build these chairs. They were supposed to get paid $2 per chair. Some days they got high and some they didn't. Guess what happened."

"They made the same number of chairs either way," Alex guessed.

"First," I said, "they went on strike to get more money per chair."

"Very funny!" said Stephanie. "You're kidding, right?"

"No," I said. "They actually went on strike twice over the 70 days of the study and got two raises."[20]

"That must have taken some motivation," said Stephanie.

"They did build fewer chairs on the days when they had to smoke marijuana. Intoxication slowed them down a bit. There weren't any other problems."

"Is that the only study?" Sebastian asked.

"In another one, guys stayed in the hospital for three months and got paid to answer questions from a textbook or do some math problems. They got high on some days and didn't on other days. There was no effect."[21]

"Even when they were high?" asked Denise.

"The problems were pretty easy," I said. "But there were no signs of amotivation." A few people nodded. "So, at least in adults, there's no evidence that marijuana messes up how hard you work or how much work you get done."

SCHOOL FAILURE

"What do you mean 'at least in adults'?" asked Alex.

"There isn't a lot of research with adolescents, but they don't handle marijuana very well. The bottom line is: Marijuana's not for kids. That's why we're here."

"Give us the dirt," said Stephanie.

"I mentioned that for college students, users have grades as good as non-users."

"Right," said Sebastian.

"Is it different for high-school kids?" asked Ada.

"I'm afraid so," I said. "High-school kids who smoke pot have lower grades than their classmates. But that's not the whole story."

"It never is!" said Kate.

"At least one study showed that the kids who used marijuana actually had lower grades all the way back in grade school."

"I hope they weren't smoking pot then," said Stephanie.

"Seems unlikely," I said. "But that would mean that students who aren't connected to school are the ones who are most likely to start smoking marijuana early."

"I follow," Stephanie added. "If they're getting bad grades, they probably think they might as well smoke."

"Could be," I said.

"Hold on," said Ricardo. "It sounds like these are the students who would probably leave school anyway."

"It's hard to tell," I said. "Wayne Hall, down in Australia, did a big review of all this research."

"What'd he say?" Ricardo asked.

"It doesn't look like there's amotivational syndrome from marijuana. It's not even clear that marijuana itself is making them leave school."

"Of course not," said Alex.

"Wait," I said. "It does seem like the ones who get high a lot are also more likely to quit. They drop out more often. It looks like they just stop valuing school. They tend to hang around other kids who don't value school, either."[22]

"So is it the pot or isn't it?" Stephanie asked.

"It might not be marijuana itself, but the context. If teens get marijuana and use it, they do end up hanging out with folks who aren't conventional. They might adopt different attitudes, think little of getting an education, and drop out."

"What are we supposed to do about that?" asked Kate.

"Do you value education?" I asked.

"Of course," said Sebastian.

"Why?"

"You can get a better job. You know more. You understand things better. It's just a better life." Sebastian held his hands out, palms up for emphasis.

"Do you tell your kids?" I asked. People were silent.

"It's obvious," said Ada. "They see me going to school."

"That's great," I said. "If they see you going to school, that's bound to help. If they see that you read good books, and get excited about ideas, and make an effort to learn, that's all got to help," I said. "But what else?"

"I guess we could tell them," Kate said.

"Again, it doesn't have to be a lecture. Opportunities will come up. Notice any?"

"Any time I do a crossword puzzle," said Elise.

"Or see some adult doing a job that a college graduate wouldn't have to do," said Ricardo.

"There's always stuff on TV and the radio," Denise added. "I just saw something about salaries for different jobs. The ones that only require a high-school diploma never pay as much."

"There you go," said Kate. "Even my kids understand cash." She looked at Stephanie and they both smiled.

"So we talked about all the different things we've heard about marijuana. We talked about the gateway theory and why it might not help our cause. We somehow turned that into how to talk about our own use. Then we talked about identifying problems," I said.

"It's been a big night," said Stephanie.

"I agree. Are your brains pretty full?"

"You bet!" said Ricardo.

"We've still got a lot of important stuff to cover," I said. "Remember to keep up the stuff from last time. Let them have their feelings. Listen and reflect. Look for opportunities to talk about drugs."

"We will. We will!" said Stephanie.

"You all sound like good parents."

CHAPTER 7: PROS, CONS AND DIFFICULT DECISIONS

People waved and nodded on their way out. I noticed that Alex was linger-ing as everyone else headed for the door. I looked up at him and raised my eyebrows.

"I had a couple of extra questions," he said.

"Shoot."

"I feel like I need to cut down a bit myself. I just get high too often. I don't want to say any prayers or anything," Alex said.

"Let's talk about it. You got a minute?"

"Definitely."

"Let's sit down," I said, motioning toward the chairs. "You know I'm not going to give you any trouble. How serious do you think this is?"

"No big deal, but I should cut down."

"How often do you get high?" I asked.

"I'm not sure exactly. It varies."

"Do you get high every night?"

"Oh, no."

"Most nights?"

"I guess so. Probably five nights a week."

"What about during the day?" I asked.

"No," he said. "I guess, um, sometimes on the weekend."

"How long have you been getting high five nights a week?"

"Gee," Alex said. "Let me think. It was after my divorce. Probably about three years."

"Did the marijuana have anything to do with the divorce?"

"Ha!" Alex said. "No. It wasn't anything that simple."

"Any other troubles? Driving high? Busted?"

"No, nothing like that," he said.

"Any memory problems? Screwups at work?"

"No."

"Do you have a cough?"

"No. I don't really have any problems with it."

"Then why change?" I asked. This was a bit of a ploy on my part, but I always want to hear people's reasons.

"I just feel like I should cut down if I'm going to tell my kids not to do it. You're the doctor. What do you think?"

"It's not about what I think; it's about what you think. This is completely your decision. I'm not going to be looking over your shoulder or making you pee in a cup."

"I hope not," said Alex.

"If things were really serious, I would want to send you to one of my buddies, a therapist in town."

"I don't think that's necessary."

"Then I'd like to walk through some steps I've used in my lab to help people change things they don't like.[23] It won't take long. Part of why I want to do it is that you could do it with your kids if they use. Or you can do the same thing with them to help them never try. Are you game?" I asked.

"Sure." Alex nodded.

I paused for a minute.

"Really," he said, "I'm game."

"I guess I'm trying to decide if I'm game myself," I said. "Sometimes I don't like doing this sort of thing because people confuse it with therapy."

"I understand," Alex said.

"If we can do this like two guys chatting, I'd feel more comfortable, and I bet you would, too."

"Yeah," Alex said. "This is hard enough. I don't want you getting all formal on me."

"Great," I said. "Usually I like to get a feel for what's good about marijuana for you personally. What are the things you like about it?"

He paused for a minute and chuckled.

"Ha! I wasn't really expecting that. I thought we'd just talk about the bad stuff."

"We'll get there," I said. I took out a pen and a pad of paper. "Just call out whatever comes to mind."

"How would I do this with my kids? I mean, if they haven't used?"

"Just ask them what reasons they've heard for trying. If you can stand the thought, ask them why they might ever try. But let's get back to you. Why do you smoke as often as you do?"

"I just like to get high," he said. "That's all there is to it."

"Okay. Is it that you like the feeling?"

"Right," he nodded. I wrote "THE FEELING."

"Are there other parts of the high that you enjoy?"

"This is weird. Why are we talking about this?" he asked.

"It just helps people understand what they really like."

"I have more fun when I'm high," he said. "Movies are funnier."

"Okay." I wrote "ENJOY MOVIES MORE." "What else?"

"I have more fun with my friends. It's just a good time hanging out," Alex added. I wrote "FUN WITH FRIENDS."

"What else?"

"That's really about it. I guess it really doesn't sound like much."

"A lot of people claim it helps them relax," I said.

"That's true. I do use it for that," he said. I wrote "RELAXATION."

"Anything else?"

"It sounds kind of funny, but it's more fun getting it on."

"I follow," I said, and wrote "SEX." "Other people say that it gives them insights or helps them with their problems."

"I don't really see it that way." He shook his head.

"And some people say it makes them more creative," I added.

"No," said Alex. "I know those guys. They think a peanut butter and baloney sandwich is creative."

I went through the list with Alex one more time, and then said, "So is that it?"

"I think so. There is one more thing. I sort of use it as a reward. It's like I reach the end of the day and want to celebrate that I made it through." He paused a minute. "I guess that sounds kind of silly. So what? I made it to the end of the day."

"It can be a big deal. You're working. You've got kids. Sometimes just making it through the day is a real achievement," I said.

"I see what you mean," he said. "Still, that doesn't mean I have to get high."

"True. Very true." I added "REWARD" to the list. "Let's talk about the things that aren't so good. What are the drawbacks?" I asked.

"I have to admit that I get paranoid sometimes. Not real bad. Sometimes people say things and I'm not sure how they mean it. I can get caught up thinking about what they said over and over."

I moved to the bottom of the page in the notebook and wrote "PARA-NOID."

"What else?" I asked.

"It's getting a little pricey. I can't get an eighth for what I used to." I wrote a big dollar sign on the next line in the notebook and waited. Alex continued, "It's just not as fun as it used to be. I can't really explain it. It used to be more special."

"Should I write 'not special'?" I asked. Alex nodded. I waited. "Is anybody asking you to quit? Are you getting in arguments with your family or friends?"

"My girlfriend and I had one talk about it. A couple of talks, actually. She wants to go out and do more stuff instead of staying in and watching TV. She's tired of being around a stoned guy all the time."

"Got you," I said. I wrote "CONFLICTS WITH GIRLFRIEND." "Anything else?"

"Nothing comes to mind."

"You said something about your kids," I stated.

"Oh! I feel sort of stupid getting high every night and then telling them not to. I don't think they know I'm high every night. I don't get high when they're staying with me, but it feels hypocritical."

"I follow," I said. I wrote "FEEL HYPOCRITICAL."

"I have to admit," Alex added. "I do end up eating more ice cream than I probably should." He patted his belly. "I'm sure the pot doesn't help." I wrote "WEIGHT GAIN."

"Anything else?"

"I think that's it," Alex said. We waited quietly. "Yes, I think that's it."

"Then I'd like to ask you to rate how important each of these is, from 1 to 10. So if 10 is really important to you and 1 is not at all important, where would you rate THE FEELING for getting high? How important is that to you?"

"Really only about a 6," Alex said. "Maybe a 7. It's important but not really important."

"Okay," I said. "So walk through all of these and give them your rating. Know what I mean?"

"Sure," Alex said. I handed him the pen and paper. He wrote numbers thoughtfully.

"It's funny," he said. "I can't quite narrow this down to a number sometimes."

"Just give it your best shot," I said. "Your first impression will do the trick." He added some more numbers. "Mind if I take a look?"

"Go to town," he said.

"I can see why you're struggling with this," I said. "The pros and cons are pretty equal."

"I do have more cons than pros," he said.

"Good point, but they're about the same value for you." We sat quietly. I thought I heard the wind at the windows.

"That's why I'm stuck," he said.

"How about this," I began, "from 1 to 10, how willing are you to quit smoking marijuana right now?"

"Like for good?"

"Yes," I said.

"Zero. I'm not willing to quit. I'm willing to cut down though."

"So this is where I can run into trouble," I said. "I feel like I'm supposed to say that quitting is the only way. I'm glad you've been so frank about it, though. Since you're really not willing to quit, we'll talk about cutting down. You can imagine how this gets me in hot water."

"I bet," he said. "But thanks for not pushing the abstinence thing. I'd never do that."

"Let's do what we can do," I said. "Okay, 1 to 10, how willing are you to cut down?" Alex scratched his cheek lightly.

"Really only about a 6. I guess it depends on what you mean by cut down."

"What do you mean by cut down?" I asked.

"Once a week. Just one weekend night a week."

"What would that be like?" I asked.

"The night I got high would be great," Alex smiled. We both laughed.

"The other nights?"

"I have my own little ritual. I usually fire up one bowl and watch a little TV before I go to sleep. It's not like I'm high at work or anything."

"I got you," I thought a few seconds and took a breath. "Then why is your girlfriend disappointed about it?"

"Sometimes it's a little early. I have to admit it. Sometimes I'm high by 8 o'clock. She thinks I'm not as good at listening to her, hearing about her day."

"What do you think?"

"That's partly true. I don't always want to hear every word everyone in her office said to everyone else. Sometimes that's easier to endure high." He paused.

"It sounds like there's another side, though."

"On the other hand, she's right. I can't always keep track of the problem. If something's really bothering her, then she's disappointed. It's a buzz kill. I don't want to hash through it all. I just tell her how to fix the problem and she doesn't get to tell her story."

"I follow," I said. "That's a bit of a guy thing. We want to fix it and they want to chat. She wants you to listen and connect and she thinks you can't do it because you're high."

"Right."

"So what would it be like if you're not getting high during the week?" I asked.

"I would end up listening better. It's true." He paused. "I bet she'd like that."

"I don't mean for this to sound like a trick, but I want you to know what we just did right here so you can do it with your kids," I said.

"I noticed you were asking lots of questions," Alex said. "I can take a lesson from that right away."

"Great," I said. "I try to ask questions that aren't going to have just 'yes' or 'no' as an answer. Everybody appreciates that, especially kids."

"It seemed like you were really listening," Alex said.

"I was."

"I guess what I'm trying to say is that it seemed to matter why I was using, not just how much."

"Thanks. I'm glad that came across. Yes, it's much more important why," I said.

"I didn't really expect to talk about the good things."

"I also asked you to elaborate on the bad things, though. Once people spend time talking about the disadvantages of getting high so much, they often realize they're more willing to change than they thought."

"I follow," said Alex. "That's just what happened to me."

"Did you feel like I was tricking you?"

"No. It's the listening. I noticed that you nod your head and lean forward and all of that, too."

"Okay," I said. "Want to give it a try this week and let me know how it's going next time?"

"Sure."

"So your goal would be to get high only once in the next seven days. Is that right?"

"Yes."

"Do you know how you would do it?"

"Just put the pipe down," Alex said. "Do other stuff. Actually, I'll do the same things I always do, but not hit the pipe."

"Is it really that simple?"

"Ha! I think so."

"What will you do when you want to get high?" I asked.

"Just wait it out." Alex thought a minute. "Truthfully, it's going to be the same sort of evening. I'm not going to get the shakes or anything."

"What will you do when it gets tough?" I asked.

"Probably just distract myself. By the time the evening rolls around, I'll just watch a little TV like any other night, but not get high."

"Can you talk about it with someone if it gets difficult?"

"My girlfriend."

"Would she be a good person to talk to?"

"Yes. I didn't mean to make her sound bad. She'll be very cool about this."

"So how confident are you that you can do it?" I asked.

"Pretty confident."

"You know," I said, "from 1 to 10."

"About an 8."

"What would it take to get it to a 9?"

"Once I go a couple of days, I'll be more confident."

"It sounds pretty good. If it's this straightforward, why didn't you do it before?"

"I guess I didn't realize why I wanted to. I didn't know how hypocritical I felt about it until we started talking. That one's important to me. I should probably change the rating on that one."

"There you go!" I said. "One thing though. Please don't skip the parenting class next week if you fall down on the smoking. I don't want you to blow it off just because you got high more times than you said. I'm not going to chew you out."

"Don't worry. I know you're not that kind of guy. I'll be here."

"Tell you what," I said, reaching for my wallet to pull out one of my cards. "Give me a call during the week if things get rough. No big deal. Just take my number and check in if you feel like you're really struggling." He put the card in his back pocket. We shook hands and headed for the door.

FIGURES FOR ALEX'S DECISIONS

THE PROS		THE CONS	
the feeling	7	paranoid	6
enjoy movies more	6	$	7
fun with friends	7	not special	7
relaxation	7	conflict with girlfriend	8
sex	7	feel hypocritical	7
reward	5	munchies/weight gain	6

CHAPTER 8: MARIJUANA AND THE TEEN BRAIN

I'd had a really busy week and honestly didn't think about the program for parents until a couple days before the next session. I did think about Alex a lot. I'm always a little conflicted about listing the pros and cons with someone in a way that seems like I'm playing therapist. I guess I should list the pros and cons of doing that myself. He seemed like he was sincerely interested in cutting down his use. There are people who really should stay away from marijuana completely. I never know who they are. They often don't know, either. If he was still having problems, I hoped he might entertain the idea of quitting. I'd also love to hook him up with a therapist in town. But he didn't seem interested. You can lead a horse to water and all that.

I reviewed my notes and realized that we were jumping around a bit, but I liked that we had discussed what was interesting to the parents at the time. The discussion of the gateway theory always gives me some hope. I'm constantly talking with parents about how to discuss their own use. It was good to see that people were so open-minded about problems, too. I arrived a little early, but people were already there and chatting away. It was nice to see folks were making friends.

"How did it go this week?" I asked.

"I was just telling Stephanie," Kate began. "I told my daughter that thing you said. You know, about the guy who told his kids he couldn't win no matter what he said about his getting high."

"What happened?"

"She applied it to everything!" Stephanie broke in. "Give a gal a hammer and the whole world's a nail."

"What do you mean?" I asked.

"I said that if I told her I never tried she wouldn't believe me and all that. She smiled and took it pretty well. But then I tried it with other stuff." Kate looked pretty pleased.

"Other drugs?" I asked.

"No." She shook her head. "Like she and her sister were fighting and I said that no matter what I said to them it would make me look bad. They already knew not to fight."

"Did it help?"

"Sort of," she said. "They worked it out themselves and I didn't have to be the mean one. I think they did it quicker than if I had yelled and screamed, too."

"Sounds great! Anybody else have something relevant happen this week?"

"I got a little lost in the gateway argument," said Ada. "I told my kids that marijuana didn't have to lead to hard stuff, but then I didn't have a lot of ammunition left for why they weren't supposed to use it."

"I still feel like we only covered what marijuana doesn't do," Alex said.

"I was going to jump through a few more myths," I said. "But it seems like we need to focus on the real negative consequences of marijuana now." People nodded. "I'm going to spend the whole time on the brain, then, if you are all game. It'll be a shorter session, but more intense."

"We're willing," said Denise.

BRAIN BASICS

"Who heard that marijuana kills brain cells?" I asked, picking up the chalk. All hands shot up. "Who believed it?" All hands went down. I moved to the board and started writing.

"This all going to be true?" Stephanie asked with a grin. I nodded.

"The first research on marijuana and the brain was done all wrong. It got a lot of news coverage anyway. It said that marijuana users had larger ventricles, the big holes inside your brain." I drew pictures of two brains as if they had been cut above eye level to reveal the ventricles inside. One had much larger ventricles than the other.

"Wasn't it true?" asked Ricardo.

"No," I said. "What would you want to know about a study like this?"

"Had they done any other drugs?" Alex asked.

"Exactly," I said. "The marijuana users had done a lot of other drugs that could have caused the larger ventricles. In addition, the researchers used a really poor way to measure the size of the ventricles."

"What?" Sebastian asked.

"It was called air encephalography." I wrote the words on the board. "They pump the fluid from your spine until it's all gone. Supposedly, more fluid meant more space in the head, so bigger holes."

"That sounds dumb," said Kate.

"We can take pictures of the brain now. You put your head in a giant magnet," I said.

"I had one of those. An MRI." Sebastian piped up.

"Magnetic resonance imaging," I said. "They redid the study with marijuana users who hadn't used other drugs. Their ventricles were the same size as everyone else's."

"So the brain is safe?" asked Stephanie.

"Hang on," I said. "There's more to it."

"There always is!" said Denise.

"It looked like marijuana didn't change the structure of the brain. At least the ventricles were fine. But this research only focused on the ventricles, and only looked at the adult brain." I went to the board and drew a couple of brains viewed from the side, a small one and a larger one.

"Until recently, everyone thought that your brain was done growing when you were 6 years old or so. That's about when your brain reaches its full size. Then the rest was just details. Now we know that's not the whole story." I drew a nerve cell on the board. "What's this?" I asked.

"A bad drawing of a nerve cell," said Elise.

"Thanks!" I smiled. "You're born with 100 billion nerve cells, or neurons, in your brain. That's 100,000,000,000." I wrote all the zeros on the board. "Each one has a cell body. It has a long axon for carrying electrical signals. It also has 10,000 little branches coming off called dendrites. The dendrites connect to other neurons. With 100 billion neurons each with 10,000 branches, you can make a lot of connections."

"A bazillion," Ricardo mumbled.

"Some connections get used a lot," I continued. "As you learn new skills, some neurons start working together more and more. Their connections get better. They really thrive." I drew another neuron next to the first and some thick, wavy lines between them. "Other connections don't fire as often. They don't get much use. They wither." I erased the lines.

"Use it or lose it," Sebastian said.

"Exactly. So even though your brain isn't getting bigger all the time, it's still making new connections as you learn. The wiring is changing all the time. Dendrites grow out and form connections and some of them stay and some of them don't."

Everyone looked intrigued.

"There are a couple of key times in life when dendrites really go wild. They spread out in all directions as much as they can, trying to make as many connections as possible." I drew dendrites sticking out all over the place on one neuron.

"Sounds cool," Stephanie said.

"One of these times is the notorious 'terrible twos.' Two-year-olds learn at an amazing rate. It seems like every day they say something new or do something new." I looked around to make sure everybody was following. "What would you guess is another time when dendrites grow like crazy?"

"Adolescence?" Elise asked.

"Yes," I said. "How'd you guess?"

"Honestly," she said, "it's a lot like the return of the terrible twos."

"You must have kids!"

"You bet!" she said.

WHITE MATTER MATTERS

"What's all this got to do with pot?" asked Elise.

"Good question," I said. "If we know that adolescence is a prime time for development, then it might be a time when the brain is very sensitive to marijuana. But first I need to explain a little more about the brain."

"Here we go!" said Alex.

"You know that a lot of the brain, especially the outside, is all gray. That's why we call it gray matter. But other parts, especially inside, are white."

"White and gray, okay," Sebastian said.

"White matter is made of the same kind of brain cells, but with a special coating, the myelin." I wrote "MYELIN" on the board and drew a coating around the neuron. "The myelin is a fatty cover. It's insulation that helps electrical signals travel faster. Faster signals mean faster thinking. White matter helps the brain work efficiently."

"Do some people not have any?" Kate joked.

"Some people sure seem like they don't have any." I smiled. "Truth is, once you reach age 50 or so, you begin to lose some." I scratched my head. "Let's just say things start slowing down then, too."

"No kidding. Sometimes even earlier than that," Alex grumbled. I walked to the other side of the board.

"The white and gray matter work together. The proportion of white and gray is important. That's how the brain gets messages across." Everyone seemed to follow, but I paused. "You with me?"

"We got it," said Stephanie. "White and gray have to be in the right proportion."

"A team or researchers at Duke University got a great idea," I said.

"You get so excited; it's funny," Denise said.

"Hey! This is what happens when you're a geek. So these Duke researchers knew that marijuana didn't seem to have any effect on brain structure in adults. They also knew that adolescence was a prime time for brain development. What would you guess they asked next?"

"Oh!" said Sebastian. "Why not look at people who smoked pot during adolescence?"

"Exactly," I said. "They took a big bunch of people who smoked marijuana. A lot of marijuana. They divided them into two groups. One group had started using weed before age 17. The others started when they were older." I drew a line down the chalkboard and wrote "YOUNGER" on one side and "OLDER" on the other. "Guess what they found?"

"Oh no!" said Ada. "Were their brains smaller?" She pointed toward the side of the board labeled "YOUNGER."

"Not quite. Nobody's whole brain was smaller. But the people who started smoking earlier had different proportions of white and gray matter. They didn't have myelin in the same places as the folks who waited to smoke pot."

"Wait a minute," said Sebastian. "What about other drugs? What about brain tumors and smacks to the head?"

"Good question," I said. "These guys at Duke know what they're doing. They excluded anyone who used a lot of other drugs. They even excluded heavy drinkers. Nobody with head injury or mental illness was allowed in the study, either."[24]

"So alcohol does mess this up!" Stephanie said. "You made me wait."

"Alcohol can shrink the whole brain, too. It's a rough drug over the years. But here we see that starting marijuana in adolescence alters the brain, too."

"Maybe the ones who started getting high when they were younger just smoked longer. Maybe it's not when you start but how long you smoke," Stephanie said.

"Good point. You're really thinking!"

"It's the white matter," she said.

"The researchers looked at the number of years that people smoked and it didn't matter. The white matter was only out of whack for folks who started young."

"Well, how much pot are these guys smoking?" asked Sebastian.

"Another good question. They were pretty serious users. They got high most days. They averaged over 100 joints per year." I could see a few people counting on their fingers.

"Okay. So what?" Denise asked. "So their brains aren't white and gray exactly right. Big deal."

"Let me explain," I said. "The people who started smoking earlier had underdeveloped white and gray matter. It looks like their brains would be less efficient. But what's also important is WHERE these differences showed up. Different parts of the brain do different things. Some parts look more sensitive to marijuana than others."

"So where were the differences?" asked Ricardo.

"One important area is at the front of the head—the frontal lobes of the brain." I pointed to my forehead. "This part is important for planning, for showing restraint." I looked around. "Who knows the name Phineas Gage?"

"Is he a brain researcher?" asked Ada.

"He's that guy who got the crowbar stuck in his head," answered Ricardo.

"Right. In the 1850s, Phineas Gage was a responsible, rational, helpful railroad worker. He was in charge of a crew that was laying train tracks. They had to blow up some rocks to lay some track. The explosion sent a tamping iron—a big piece of metal—into the front of his head."

"That's so gross!" Denise said, tossing down her pen.

"He survived," I said. "He lived anyway, but he didn't act the same. What happened?"

"He started cussing and crap like that!" Ricardo blurted.

"Exactly. The tamping iron had damaged the frontal lobe. He lost his ability to inhibit himself. He started acting on his first impulse. He couldn't hold the same job, didn't have the same relationships with his family. He got himself in plenty of trouble." I wrote "GAGE" on the board.

"It's a big jump to say what the frontal lobes do based on one weird guy," said Alex.

"I agree. But there's been a lot of research since then. Several groups of people have problems with the frontal lobes. Hyperactive kids. Impulsive people in general. And of course, substance abusers. People who can't inhibit their first response."

"I get it," Stephanie said.

"Okay," I said. "If marijuana is altering the frontal lobe, we've got the potential for a real vicious circle here. This is the part of the brain that would normally help you stay away from drugs. Yet the drug is actually altering that part. In theory, that might make you more likely to use again."

"Do they?" asked Alex.

"People who start using marijuana younger are more likely to run into problems. Generally, the earlier you start smoking pot, the more likely you are to get in trouble with it."

"Are there any other brain studies that show differences from pot, or just this one?" asked Alex.

"Good question. You might think that one study is just a fluke. But another group of researchers at Johns Hopkins University and the National Institute on Drug Abuse found similar results. They only looked at men. They compared guys who got high four times a week to guys who had

never gotten high. They found that the guys who got high also had proportions of white and gray matter that were different. The difference was particularly big at the hippocampus.[25] What's the hippocampus do?"

"It helps memory!" Ricardo said.

"Exactly. Given marijuana's impact on memory, this result shouldn't be
a giant surprise."

"You said in your book that marijuana doesn't hurt memory except
when you're high," Denise said.

"Wow! I'm flattered that you read my book," I said. Denise looked
down. "It's true. People who are high can't learn new material, but once
they're down their memories work. All that research is on adults, though.[26]
We don't really know about teens."

"Well, does this brain stuff turn into anything that matters? Does all this
gray and white change the way your brain really works?" Alex asked.

I glanced at my watch.

"The bottom line is: Your brain is important and you only get one.
Adolescence is a big time for brain development. People who smoke pot
during adolescence have changes in their brain structures. Some of these
changes are in the frontal lobe, an important part of the brain for planning
and organization. Remember Phineas Gage."

"This is getting kind of intense," Denise said.

"I agree. I'd like to get into the brain-function stuff. It's one thing to say
that the brain changes shape, but that actually means something for how
the brain works. Are you guys with me?"

"Can we take a break a minute?" asked Kate.

"Absolutely!" I knew this material was dense and wanted to give everybody a chance at it.

CHAPTER 9: MARIJUANA AND BRAIN FUNCTION

When everyone returned, I saw an unfamiliar face. A bearded guy in a flannel shirt sat beside Kate. I just couldn't place him.

"I'm sorry," I said. "I don't know your name. I was just talking about memory, too."

"Oh! I'm Rob. Sorry I'm late. I just got off work. I hear you were talking about some cool stuff. I wanted to sit in. You mind?"

"The more the merrier," I said, handing him a name tag. "Glad to hear word's getting out."

"Can you sum up a little?" asked Ada.

"Of course," I said. "The bottom line is: Teens shouldn't smoke pot. Although adult users don't show any changes in the shape of their brains, folks who start using early in life have different brain structures from folks who start later or never start."

"I see," she said. "Thanks."

"I want to move on to how marijuana alters the way the brain actually works. We'll also walk through a study about teen use lowering intelligence, just to answer Stephanie's questions."

"I'm not the only one!"

"Of course. We'll answer anybody's questions about how this brain structure translates into something that matters. Okay?" Everybody looked up. They all seemed ready to go.

"You guys are right in the thick of it," said Rob.

"You bet! We've got different ways to see how the brain works now. They're getting better and better. We can take pictures with the MRI, like Sebastian talked about. These pictures show a lot about the shape of the brain and the size of different parts."

"Sounds cool," Rob said.

"We can even take a movie of the brain this way, to see how it actually functions." I wrote "MRI" on the board and then "fMRI." "The 'f' is for 'functional.' Functional MRI tells us how the brain works."

"Is this on the test?" Stephanie asked. Everybody grinned.

"We also have PET scans. Positron emission tomography. You inject the person with a radioactive substance and the machine can track the radioactivity in the blood. You can see where the blood goes in the brain during different tasks." I wrote "PET" on the board.

"Is that those colored pictures?" asked Sebastian. I nodded.

"Another way to see how the brain works requires lots of little sensors attached to the scalp. These little electrodes amplify the signals underneath the skull. What's this called?"

"EEG," said Ricardo.

"Yes. The electroencephalograph." I wrote the word on the board. "All of these reveal that marijuana changes the way the brain works during intoxication. They also show that heavy use is not a good idea." I wrote "HEAVY USE" and drew a line through it.

"How much is heavy?" asked Denise.

"We'll talk about it as we go," I said. "First, let's talk about the high brain. Let's look at how the brain works during intoxication." I drew a side view of a brain on the board. "When someone smokes marijuana, it goes directly to the lungs. Where does the blood go from there?"

"The brain and the heart," Alex said.

"You got it. Marijuana doesn't change the total amount of blood in the brain. But it does change where that blood goes." I drew a simple brain stem. "Here's the brain stem. It's sometimes called the reptilian brain. It handles all the functions of your basic reptile: eating, sleeping, running away from bigger reptiles, that sort of thing. It's your life-support system. If something happens to your brain-stem, you're in trouble."

"Marijuana doesn't do anything like that!" said Denise.

"You're right," I said. I drew a ring around the brain-stem. "There's a ring of brain tissue around the brain-stem that's very important. The Latin word for 'ring' is 'limbus.' This is called the 'limbic' system. What does it involve?"

"Emotion," shouted Sebastian.

"Yes," I said. "The limbic system is often called 'the seat of emotion.' That's a bit oversimplified. The limbic system handles all kinds of feelings, but also motivation, and certain aspects of memory. As you can imagine, the limbic system develops a lot during adolescence. Adolescence is when your emotions go wild."

"No kidding," Stephanie said.

"That hormonal emotional roller coaster is training the limbic system to handle your feelings," I said. "You're developing controls over your emotions as your brain gets more efficient. It's more complicated than that, but you get the idea."

"I hate this," said Alex, folding his arms across his chest. "I hate this pretending like the brain is all these different parts, that one part does one thing and one part does another. And that's your whole life."

"I agree," I said. "I don't mean to make it sound like your whole life boils down to neurons going snap, crackle and pop."

"Yeah!" Sebastian said.

"Your brain is all connected, though. It's just easier for us to talk about it if we break it into sections." I paused and looked around. "You with me?" I asked Alex. He nodded.

"The limbic system has parts involved with emotion. It's also important for memory. The hippocampus is in the limbic system and it's essential for remembering. Marijuana makes you happy and it wrecks your memory, so of course the limbic system is involved."

"Like I said, though, you said in your book that people who smoke a lot don't show memory problems," Denise said.

"Only adults, and only when they're straight," I said. "When people are high, their memory for new material is not as good. In truth, for some people, it's not very good at all."[27]

"Um, I know this guy who says his memory's fine while he's high," she added.

"Was the guy named Denise?" I asked. Everyone smiled. "Seriously, remote memory is fine. Your memory for things you've already learned isn't going to disappear while you're high. You're not going to forget your phone number or your first-grade teacher's name."

"What was your first-grade teacher's name?" Stephanie asked.

"I'm not high," I smiled. "My first-grade teacher was Mrs. Loiterstein. She was great. There isn't enough pot in the world to make me forget her." I paused and looked around. Everyone seemed to follow. "But you're not going to read something high and remember it well. You're not going to learn calculus formulas while you're high and remember them as well as you would've if you weren't high."

"Is all this stuff in your book?" Ada asked.

"Down to the last gory detail," I said.

I wrote "REMOTE MEMORY" on the board with a circle around it. Then I wrote "NEW MEMORIES" and put a line through it. "Remote memory is fine. Forming new memories is impaired while you're high." Denise and several others wrote in their notebooks. "So where was I?" I asked. They grinned.

"Pot on the brain," said Stephanie with a giggle.

"So we see that the total blood flow in the brain is the same while you're high, but it goes to different places. It goes to the limbic system, which explains some of marijuana's mood effects. But if there's more blood there, there's less blood in other places."

"Like where?" Sebastian asked.

"It depends on what your brain is doing. Suppose you're supposed to listen to tones and count certain ones. Normally, you'd get more blood going to the sides of the brain, the parts involved in hearing and the parts important for attention."[28]

"The temporal lobes?" asked Ricardo.

"Exactly. But when you're high, guess what happens?"

"The blood doesn't go there," Bev said.

"You got it," I said. "High people have a harder time getting blood to the parts of the brain that help attention."

"Marijuana makes it hard to pay attention. I could've told you that," Stephanie said.

"Now we've confirmed Stephanie's clinical impressions," I said. "A lot of science is proving for sure what everybody already knows. But we've got evidence here that the attention probably comes from different blood flow in the brain."

"Any other parts not getting blood?" asked Sebastian.

"The frontal lobe. Like we talked about."

"Back to Phineas Gage?" asked Ada.

"I'm not saying high people act like Phineas Gage. But the frontal lobe is important for planning. It helps people inhibit. And it's not getting the same amount of blood high as straight. A few studies suggest that people have trouble inhibiting when they're high, too."

"Like inhibiting how much you eat!" said Sebastian, patting his stomach.

"That's another mechanism," I said. "But even studies with adults show that people have some trouble inhibiting when they're high."

"How do they measure that?" asked Alex. I went to the board with my white chalk and wrote the word "BLACK" in big, bold, white letters.

"Okay," I said. "I'm going to ask a question and you need to answer as fast as you can. Ready?"

"Yes," they said.

"What color is that word?"

"BLACK!" they yelled.

"No," I said. "The color of the word is white. You read the word instead of saying the color. That's called the Stroop effect, named after the guy who discovered it. We all have much more practice reading words than naming their colors. You have to inhibit reading the word 'BLACK' to say the color 'WHITE.' It's hard now. As you can imagine, high people take even longer to say the color. It's just harder to inhibit."[29]

"Anything else?" asked Alex.

"One more thing about the high brain comes from EEG studies. This is a little complicated, but I think you can handle it."

"Thanks for the vote of confidence," Kate said sarcastically.

"The main point of this work is that when you're high, it's more difficult to separate what's important from what's not important. It's harder to see what's relevant and what's irrelevant. Get it?"

"How about an example?" Sebastian asked.

"Let me explain one of the tasks that people do when they've got the EEG electrodes on their heads. Imagine you're going to hear a bunch of tones. Some are high and some are low. Some are short and some are long. Whenever you hear a long, high tone, you're supposed to press a button. Get it?"

"Okay," Ada mumbled.

"Your brain waves are interesting on a task like this. When the long, high tone happens, the target tone, the one you're supposed to look for, your brain emits a big wave." I went to the board and drew a line that went up and then down again. "It's as if your brain is saying, 'That's it. That's the one I'm looking for!' Okay?"

"We get you," said Stephanie.

"In contrast, if it's not the tone you're looking for, your brain waves don't do anything special. Your brain is saying that it's business as usual, no need to pay attention." Everyone seemed to follow. I drew a straight, horizontal line next to the wave I'd drawn before.

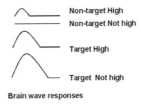

Non-target High
Non-target Not high

Target High

Target Not high

Brain wave responses

"What happens when you're high?" asked Alex.

"The high brain gets these a little confused. The wave in response to the target tone is a little smaller." I drew a wave adjacent to the first one, but it didn't go up as high. Then I drew a horizontal line next to the previous one, but put a little bump going up and down near the center. "And the wave in response to the non-target tones is a little bigger."

"It's like you can't tell them apart," said Stephanie.

"Well," I said, "it's as if your brain is having a harder time telling them apart and works less efficiently."[30]

"Was this done in kids?" asked Ada.

"No," I chuckled. "Ethics committees aren't about to let anybody give marijuana to kids in the laboratory. This work was done in adults. The effect might be even larger in adolescents. We just don't know."

"Well, does it all go back to normal when you're down?" asked Denise.

"Good question," I said. "Let's review a second before we move to the chronic effects. We can see that the high brain has different patterns of blood flow and different brain-wave patterns. The results suggest that the high brain works less efficiently, and has a harder time paying attention. The high brain also has less action in the frontal lobes, where all your good planning and inhibiting skills are."

AFTER THE HIGH IS GONE

"Okay. Okay," said Denise. "But is it permanent?"

"A few things that happen in the high brain seem to stay the same with chronic use. Other things seem to go in the opposite direction, as if your brain is trying to compensate for being high all the time."

"Like what?" Sebastian asked.

"Let me give a couple of caveats first. This work was done on adults. We don't always know when they first started getting high. The impact on adolescents is probably even more dramatic. So let's keep that in mind."

"Okay. Okay," said Denise again.

"I also need to emphasize that some of these effects are small. They're nowhere near as bad as changes in the brain related to alcoholism or a swift kick in the head." I went to the board and wrote "SMALL EFFECTS." "The first results have to do with blood flow. Some studies show that chronic users have less blood flow to the brain than non-users."[31]

"Whoa! Whoa!" said Denise. "Who's a chronic user?"

"All of these studies focused on people who got high every day for at least six months." The room was quiet. A few people seemed to be count-ing on their fingers again.

"All of these studies. You mean there's more than one?" Sebastian asked.

"Yes. A couple studies show less blood in the brain directly. A couple more studies show decreased metabolism in the brain for chronic users. These support the idea that long-term use decreases brain activity."

"Why didn't they tell us this stuff before?" Stephanie asked. "Or was that what they meant about killing brain cells?"

"It's not killing brain cells. Let me explain. The brain seems to adapt. Guess what happens to blood flow when these people smoke pot?"

"It gets worse?" asked Ada.

"No," I said. "It goes back to normal. When they get high the blood flow to the brain increases."[32]

"How does that work?" asked Kate.

"We're not sure. It's as if the marijuana is increasing blood flow to the brain. So every time you smoke it, your body tries to compensate. Your body knows that marijuana is going to increase the blood flow, so it closes down the pathways a little. You know, it tries to keep things in balance."

"That's weird," said Denise.

"It's not that uncommon. Your body does whatever it can to overcome the impact of drugs. Alcohol increases your heart rate. But if you give somebody the cues for alcohol, like one of those non-alcoholic beers, his heart rate will DECREASE. I've done this in my laboratory and lots of other folks have, too. It's as if your body is saying, 'Here comes that alcohol. It's going to crank up my heart, so let's slow it down to get ready.'"[33]

"So it's the same for pot and the blood in your brain?" Sebastian asked.

"Looks like it. Your brain takes steps to keep the blood flow from getting excessive during the high. But then, after decreasing the blood flow over and over for months, the blood flow ends up decreased even when there's no marijuana in the system."

"Dude, that is a trip," Rob said. Everyone smiled.

"You can imagine what kind of arguments this can make in therapy," I said. "Somebody comes to me and claims that marijuana helps him think better. He's probably right. It's returning the blood flow in his brain back to normal. When he gives it up he's getting less blood in his head. That's got to feel fuzzy and weird."

"Can it go back to normal?" Sebastian asked.

"I hate to get into it," I said.

"Oh, come on!" Christine said.

"I don't want to lull anybody into thinking that they can smoke up for years and just spring back to normal in no time. But one study did show some improvement after 28 days of abstinence. The pot smokers still had less brain activity than the non-smokers, but it was better than it was when they were first tested, after only one day of abstinence."

"So less blood in the brain. What else?" Alex asked.

"The EEG data are also pretty discouraging. The brain waves that were messed up during intoxication seem messed up the same way in chronic users."

"That target tone stuff you were just talking about?" asked Kate.

"Right. There's supposed to be a big response to the target-tone and no response to the non-target tone. When people are high, the target response gets smaller and the non-target response gets bigger. For chronic users, it gets that way even when they're not high. They also don't do as good a job at pressing the button."

"That's messed up," said Denise with a frown.

"Does it come back?" asked Sebastian.

"Again," I said. "I don't want to lull anybody into a false sense of security. One study did show some improvement after a month of abstinence. It didn't get all the way back to normal, but it was headed in the right direction."

"So, less blood in the brain and messed-up brainwaves. Fine. But what does all that mean, really?" asked Alex. "So your brain doesn't snap, crackle and pop the same way. So what?"

"Well, it might translate into something very important. If everybody's with me so far, we can talk about the intelligence work," I said.

"Let us have it," said Stephanie.

CHAPTER 10: MARIJUANA AND INTELLIGENCE

I went to the board and wrote "IQ" in big letters. "We've seen that marijuana use in adolescence can change the structure of the brain. We've also seen that heavy use can change brain structure and function even in adults. Everybody with me?" Everyone nodded. "Now Alex asked the most relevant question of all: So what?" I looked over at Alex and he nodded.

"He's not the only one who wants to know," Elise piped up.

"Here's what," I said. "The bottom line is, teens who smoke pot lose IQ points over time."

"That's unbelievable," said Denise.

"Let me explain the whole study before everybody starts freaking out," I said. "I'll be the first one to tell you that IQ tests are not perfect. But smart people have an easier time in the world."

"That's for sure!" Ricardo said.

"How would you know?" Christine asked, hitting him on the arm.

"It's true," I said. "Folks with higher IQ scores have a higher quality of life. They are less likely to die before they reach age 65. They're less likely to develop some forms of mental illness. They have an easier time finding rewarding jobs. They're more likely to find smart partners to marry."[34]

"Not always," said Stephanie with a smile.

"If you had the chance to pick your own IQ," I said, "by all means you should pick a high one. Intelligence is worth preserving." I went to the board and wrote "HIGHER IS BETTER."

"You mean higher IQ is better," said Ricardo. "Not getting higher is better."

"Oh, yes," I said. "Now the old data on marijuana and IQ really didn't show any links. Most samples of regular users had IQ scores around 100, just like everybody else."

"Is 100 average?" asked Sebastian.

"Right," I said. "A few studies showed small differences between users and non-users, but that didn't really tell us much. Why not?"

"They could have had lower IQ scores before they started smoking pot," said Kate.

"Exactly. So how could we find out if marijuana hurt IQ?"

"We'd have to test kids when they were little," said Ada, "before they started smoking. Then we'd have to wait until some of them started getting high and test again."

"You've got it," I said. "Does everybody follow? We want to see everybody's intelligence before they ever get high and compare it to after they start using. Ideally, we'd have a control group of people the same age with the same IQ scores to compare them to. Get it?" Everybody nodded.

"How the heck are you going to do that?" asked Stephanie.

"It's not easy," I said, "but one research team has finally done it. Peter Fried at Carleton University in Ottawa started a research project years ago. He studied pregnant women to see if their behaviors altered the development in their kids. Then he studied the kids extensively." I wrote "FRIED" on the board. A couple people laughed. I must have looked perplexed.

"He studies marijuana and his name is Fried!" Kate said.

"His name's Earleywine and he studies alcohol," Stephanie said and pointed at me.

"You should see the cocaine research by Fred Blow," I added. They laughed.

"Are you making that up?" Kate asked.

"No," I said.

"That sounds pretty cool," said Denise.

"Okay. Okay. Back to the Ottawa research project," I continued. "It was a ton of hard work. You can imagine. When these kids were between 9 and 12 years old, he gave them all a very thorough assessment of intelligence. Hardly any of them had tried marijuana at the time, and none of them were using regularly. So this test was a good measure of IQ before exposure to pot. No other study has done such a superb job."[35]

"So how'd it turn out?" asked Sebastian.

"So now it's eight years later. The kids are 17 through 21. They come back to the laboratory and take an IQ test again. By this time, some of them had never smoked marijuana regularly, some were using, but less than five joints per week, and another group smoked five joints a week or more." I went to the board and wrote "NONE," "LIGHT" and "HEAVY" in three columns.

"Okay," said Denise. "Give us the bad news."

"You can see where I'm going," I said. "The heavy users had IQ scores that were five points lower than the non-users."

"What's that mean in English?" asked Ricardo.

"This was a pretty smart sample. The non-users had an average IQ of 115. That's smarter than about 85 percent of people."

"What about the users?" asked Alex.

"Their average IQ score was 110. That's still smarter than the average bear. Their scores were higher than about 75 percent of people. But that's significantly lower than their buddies who didn't smoke pot."

"Wait," said Stephanie. "Did they all have the same IQ scores before, back when they were 9? Or did the dummies just turn into the ones who smoked pot?"

"Good question. They weren't different before they started smoking pot. Only after. That's what's interesting," I said. "Usually IQ stays the same throughout your life. Unless you have a head injury or lead poisoning or something, IQ is pretty stable. But the heavy users in this study lost four IQ points over the eight years. Their peers had slight increases over the years. That's saying something."

"Was it a certain part of the IQ test?" asked Alex. "I mean, it shouldn't hurt material they learned before they started getting high. They didn't forget vocabulary words or anything, did they?"

"Does everybody understand what Alex is getting at?" I asked. "Do you think these heavy users lost vocabulary?"

"No," Kate answered.

"What do you think was most affected?" Everyone thought quietly before jumping in with answers. It was fun to see them really thinking.

"Memory!" said Stephanie.

"You got it!" I said. "Processing speed, too. How can I explain that in English?" I glanced at Ricardo. "IQ measures that required faster performance really showed differences."

Elise shook her head. "What are you thinking, Elise?" I asked.

"Marijuana makes you stupid," she said, shaking her head more. "Marijuana makes you stupid. I just can't believe it." She looked sad.

"I'm not saying you're going to wake up retarded if you try it one time. But these were some smart kids. The effect might be worse on folks with average IQ."

"What if you're already stupid?" asked Kate.

"Then your life's hard enough," I said. "Don't make things worse."

"Does it go back to normal if you quit?" Sebastian asked.

"You keep hoping!" I joked. "Again, I don't want to lull you guys into a false sense of security. Dr. Fried did have a group of kids who had used a lot but then quit for three months. Their scores were closer to the non-users than the heavy users."

"Three months!" Rob blurted.

"Yes," I said. "I know that might sound like a long time." Nobody said a word.

"Why didn't they tell us this when we were in junior high?" asked Denise. "Why'd they tell us all those lies about motivation instead?"

"These data are brand new. Nobody knew this stuff when you were in junior high." I paused to let everything sink in. I made eye contact with a few folks. "Would you have believed it at the time?" Everyone was silent.

"Maybe. If they hadn't told me that marijuana was going to make my testicles shrink, I probably would have bought it," said Alex.

"Somebody told you that marijuana would shrink your testicles?"

"Yes. Our gym coach came to our class all dressed up in a suit. We hardly recognized him. He blew up this balloon and then let the air out and said, 'This is what's going to happen to your balls!'" Alex said.

"Hang on." I smiled and chuckled. "That's an effect of steroids. The thing with the balloon was part of a steroid-prevention program. Steroids really do that. Sounds like he got confused. Are you sure it wasn't a steroid presentation?"

"No. He said pot. I remember it," Alex said. "Our gym teacher wasn't exactly the sharpest tool in the shed."

"We'll get back to this," I said. "I can't imagine you all are feeling particularly sharp now, either."

"You said it," Stephanie said.

"We covered a big world tonight. Thanks for hanging in there. If all you remember is that marijuana hurts the development of the brain in teens, that's great. We've got real proof now. Heavy use is hard on brain function, even in adults. You've got more ammunition than ever before. Feel free to share it."

"We'll spread the word," said Stephanie. And off they went.

FOLLOWING UP ON DIFFICULT DECISIONS

Alex lingered behind as other folks left.

"I wanted to ask how things were going," I said. "But I didn't want you to feel like I was breathing down your neck."

"Okay if I sit down?"

"Absolutely," I said. "Close the door first, if you like." Alex closed the door, sat down and sighed.

"I didn't quite make the goal," he said. I waited. He didn't say anything more.

"What was the goal again?"

"Only get high one night for the week."

"So how many times did you get high?"

"I was going great until the weekend came, but then I got high Friday and Saturday." He looked down.

"So instead of getting high one night, you got high two nights," I reflected. I tried to keep my tone as neutral as possible, but I thought this was incredible progress. "How do you feel about it?"

"Not so great," Alex said.

"I'm trying to get to real feelings, like we talked about the first day of the class. 'Not so great' isn't really a feeling. 'Sad, mad, glad, afraid, disappointed...,' those are feelings."

"I'm mad at myself for doing it."

"And we talked a little about soft emotions that first day. Ring a bell?"

"I didn't really understand that part. What's that got to do with my smoking too much?" he asked.

"I'm on your side," I said. "The soft emotions are the ones that are often underneath the big, butch, hard emotions like anger." We were both quiet. "But first off, you got high almost every day for three years, then you go five days without getting high and you act like it's some kind of disaster." We were quiet again. Alex looked out the window and then back at me.

"I didn't really think about it like that," he said. "You're right, though. You're right."

"So you set a goal, a really good one, and you didn't quite make it."

"Right," he nodded.

"But you got high less than you have in three years!"

"Right," he said. "You're right." It was starting to sink in. "I thought you were going to tell me I was in denial and needed to quit for good."

"There are plenty of folks who would do that," I said. "If you want somebody to jump up and down and tell you you've got a disease, I'm not the guy."

"Good."

"What was it like those five nights? How did you do it?" I asked.

"Well, I certainly wasn't going to get high that night that we talked," Alex began.

"So you started right away," I said. "That's really cool!"

"We had just talked about it," he said.

"I still want to emphasize how great that is, though," I said. "Lots of folks would've gotten high that night and made some excuse. You know, like they were saying good-bye to it or something. I think you really deserve credit."

"Okay. Thanks." He paused. "I guess that was pretty cool of me after all."

"It just shows that you're serious," I said. "It makes it easier. What else happened?"

"The next night I was really busy and sort of never got around to it, so it wasn't that hard."

"So you weren't craving or freaking out or anything?" I laughed.

"No," Alex chuckled back. "The next night I actually got into a nice conversation with my girlfriend. By the time we were through it was really time for bed, so I didn't bother."

"And you slept okay?" I asked.

"Sure. That's never a problem."

"What about the other nights?"

"I was going to watch a movie but I decided to read instead. I had stopped reading at night because I was high and knew I wouldn't remember anything. I forgot how much I like reading for pleasure," Alex said.

"Great," I said. "What were things like the next morning?"

"Gee," Alex began. "I didn't really think about it. I'm not really a morning person." He scratched his chin. "Now that you mention it, I didn't drink as much coffee. I could actually function when I first got up." He thought some more. "I never really thought about pot giving you a hangover."

"I don't think it's like that," I said. "Research doesn't really support the idea of a marijuana hangover. But it's nice to hear you've got a little more spring in the morning. Maybe it's the pot. Maybe not."

"That's cool," he said. "Ha! Something to add to the plus side of the list."

"So what happened on the weekend?"

"Friday was supposed to be my night, so I got a movie and got high and really enjoyed it."

"Did you notice any drop in tolerance?" I asked.

"I didn't really get all that high. It's funny, I guess. I just didn't get all that high. I did one good hit out of the vaporizer. I used to do three."

"Glad to hear you're vaporizing," I said. "So what happened Saturday, the night you got high when you weren't going to?"

"It's hard to explain." Alex put his hand to his face. "I had the kids for the weekend and things were going really well. I sort of wanted to celebrate. I had gotten them to bed and we had gone to the mall and we were all getting along so well. I don't know what happened."

"Was it sort of automatic?" I asked.

"In a way. I don't really remember thinking about it or deciding to get high. They had gone to bed and I had left the vaporizer and stuff out from the night before. I just hit it as a reflex, I guess. It was sitting right there."

"So how was it?"

"Kind of a drag, actually. I hadn't meant to get high and then I was. I sat there getting paranoid and mad at myself and blew my buzz. Stupid." Alex shook his head.

"So it wasn't fun anyway?"

"I just got mad at myself."

"That's what I was trying to say before about the soft emotions," I said. "A lot of times there's a softer feeling underneath that. It's easy for two butch guys like me and you to say how mad we are."

"That's true."

"But I wonder if on top of that, or underneath it, you weren't disappointed."

"I was," Alex nodded. "I was disappointed. In truth, I was a little afraid, too. I had gone all those days in a row and then I got high and then I was high again the next night."

"I think I follow, but what do you mean?"

"It was like I got high one night and then here I was getting high the next night without even thinking," he said.

"So you'd done a good job staying away, but when you came back it was hard to stay away again."

"It wasn't even hard," Alex said. "It just happened like a reflex. I didn't even get the chance to think about it."

"Would it be easier to just quit?" I asked.

"I don't think so." Alex paused. "I don't want to do that."

"You mentioned that you left everything out. Was that part of it?"

"I think so. It's dumb to leave stuff out anyway. I should have put everything away."

"If you hadn't had everything out, do you think you would've gotten high automatically on Saturday?"

"I don't think so," said Alex.

"Do you want to try again this week?"

"I'm already on track again. It's just a matter of making it through the weekend."

"So you've done better than you have in years. Now there's just a little extra step to take. Think you can do it?"

"Yes," Alex nodded. "Yes, I can."

"Other professionals would say that you need to quit for good. They'd say that since you didn't reach your goal, you must not be able to."

"I don't think that's the case," he said. "It was just one slipup. I've done better than I have in a long time, like you said. I want to try it again."

"Sounds good," I said. "Are you snowing me? Is this really how it happened?"

Alex looked surprised. "This is the real deal," he said.

"So you used less than you have in years. You had a nice time with your girlfriend, read for pleasure and didn't really suffer even though you weren't high. Your mornings seemed a little easier, too."

"Right," Alex said.

"So keep it up! Sounds like you've got nothing to lose."

"I'll see you next week," he said. I just smiled and waved.

CHAPTER 11: MORE TROUBLE FOR TEENS WHO USE MARIJUANA

The week flew by. I'd had some good things happen. A paper I'd written about marijuana and depression had finally come out. My buddy Ken Aarons had written a little newspaper story about it, and it landed on the front page of the *Albany Times Union*. Marijuana didn't seem to cause depression in my data, and I had hoped that people would focus on things that mattered more. I was really happy. Other professors had ribbed me a bit, but it was all in good fun.

The crowd had gathered by the time I arrived, even though I came early. Everyone chatted away. Then I saw that someone had a newspaper.

MENTAL ILLNESS

"You're not making our lives any easier with this stuff!" Stephanie held up the front page.

"No need to kill the messenger," I said.

"My son brought it to me," said Ricardo.

"At least he's reading the news," I said.

"I turned it into a chance to talk about the brain," he said. "It actually went pretty well."

"What did he say?" asked Kate.

"Not much," Ricardo said. "But I could tell it got him thinking."

"So we know you think there's no connection with depression." Ada motioned toward the paper. "But what's all this schizophrenia business in the news?"

"Do you want to get into that?" I asked. People nodded. I started counting on my fingers. "There are at least four decent studies that are relevant. It's kind of complicated."

"It always is!" said Kate.

"In big groups of people who started smoking marijuana early in life, a subset of them seem more likely to develop some symptoms of schizophrenia."

"What do you mean?" asked Sebastian.

"Let me give an example. One study in New Zealand showed that people who smoked pot were more likely to report schizophrenia symptoms like hearing voices or feeling paranoid. But it was only happening to folks with a special gene, and then only if they smoked pot at least once a month before they were 18."[36]

"Feeling paranoid? That could be from just getting high," Alex said.

"Good point," I said. "They didn't count it if you were on drugs at the time."

"But they're doing something illegal," said Ricardo. "That could make anybody paranoid even when they're not high."

"You're all turning into good critics of research," I said. "I know this study's not perfect. But there are three more that suggest early use increases schizophrenia symptoms. The bottom line is that I don't think marijuana causes schizophrenia"

"Why not?" asked Bev. "If there are four studies?"

"Let me explain. I think that marijuana might make people who are already at risk for schizophrenia get their first symptoms younger. But there don't seem to be more schizophrenics when pot is more popular."

"What do you mean?" asked Sebastian.

"Schizophrenia's not very common. It's always found in less than 1 percent of the population. If marijuana caused schizophrenia, they should increase together. In the 1970s, when practically everybody smoked, there weren't more schizophrenics. Countries that have high rates of marijuana use have about 1% rates of schizophrenia, just like countries that have low rates."

"Well, what are we supposed to tell our kids?" asked Ada.

"The problem is that schizophrenia's so rare. Nobody believes they're going to become schizophrenic, and 99 percent of the time they're right."

"But what about that 1 percent?" asked Kate.

"If you've got schizophrenia in the family, or any mental illness really, you might be able to make a good argument. Marijuana would be hard on the mental health for any teen. The same is true for alcohol, too much caffeine and all kinds of things."

"You don't sound too convinced," said Alex.

"It's just so alarmist." I shrugged. "You can't tell them that marijuana's going to make them go crazy when they've got friends who get high who clearly aren't crazy. I just think we can make better arguments."

"Like the brain stuff?" asked Sebastian.

"Exactly."

"But this new marijuana," Ada began. "You know, I heard on the radio that it's stronger now."

POTENCY

"What's up with this potency business?" I asked.

"It's not your father's marijuana," said Ricardo with a grin.

"It better not be my marijuana," said Alex. Kate and Stephanie both turned and looked at him.

"Nobody needs to make any confessions," I said. "How much stronger is marijuana supposed to be now? What have you heard?"

"Ten times stronger!" Alex cried out.

"Twenty times stronger," said Ada.

"Do I hear 100?" I asked. Everyone was quiet. "No takers?"

"That's too much of a stretch," said Stephanie.

"In 1984, Don MacDonald said that pot was 100 times stronger than in the 1970's."

"That's over 20 years ago!" said Ada.

"This potency argument is old," I said. "You think your kids are the first generation to get warnings about the new superpot?"

"I guess not," said Bev.

"So let me walk through this. There's a potency monitoring project at the University of Mississippi. They've been analyzing confiscated pot since the 1970's."

"What did they find?" asked Alex.

"What's the active ingredient in marijuana?" I asked.

"THC," came the resounding reply.

"Good. Tetrahydrocannabinol. Back in the day, we didn't understand THC very well. For one thing, it breaks down in the heat. That's why old pot gets weaker."

"Now he tells us!" said Sebastian.

"You can imagine what happened to the marijuana that police confiscated. It would sit in a hot evidence locker until the end of the month. Then they'd ship it down to Mississippi to have it analyzed. By the time it reached there, it had gotten pretty weak."

"How weak?" asked Denise.

"The estimates from back then put THC concentrations around 1 percent to 2 percent," I explained. "But laboratory work shows that when people smoke pot that's 1 percent THC they don't get high. They just get a headache and think they've gotten the placebo weed."

"So it broke down during storage?" asked Sebastian.

"Looks like it," I said. "So it's hard to guess how much THC there was in the marijuana at the time."

"What about today?" Stephanie asked.

"There's a lot of range. Some confiscated marijuana is still only about 2 percent THC. The averages lately are more like 4 percent to 6 percent."

"That's stronger!" Ada said.

"It looks like instead of 100 times stronger, like some people once said, we've got an average increase of twice or three times the strength," I said.

"I heard that the Dutch pot is something like 20 percent," Alex said.

"That's true," I nodded. "They've got hash that's about 40 percent THC, too. The question is: Is stronger pot more dangerous? What do you think?"

"You don't smoke as much," Bev said. "My dad talks about sitting around in the old days smoking a whole joint by himself. Now there's this one-hit pot that does the job."

"That's true," I said. "Researchers at UCLA had people smoke marijuana that was 2 percent THC and marijuana that was 4 percent THC. The folks with the 4 percent THC took smaller, shorter hits automatically. They stored less tar and junk on their lungs, too."[37]

"How did they know?" Sebastian asked.

"Any inhaled drug takes effect quickly," I said. "It doesn't take long for the blood to go from your lungs to your brain. It's not like alcohol, where you have to wait half an hour to see how drunk you are."

"Don't people just end up completely baked?" asked Elise.

"When you look at surveys that ask people how high they get, they report the same things they did years ago. The amount of time spent high and the intensity of the high hasn't really changed."

"I know it's not like it was in the 80's," said Alex. "The pot is much stronger now."

"It really is twice as strong or so," I said. "But, I should add, we're older now. The older we get the more sensitive we get to some drugs. There was a big range of what was going around back then, and there's a big range now."

"I agree," Alex said. "But I don't want my kids stumbling on some wonder pot for their first time. The thought just freaks me out."

"Then you can tell them," I said. "Does the thought of stronger marijuana make teens stay away?"

"Yeah, sure," Kate said sarcastically.

"One night of lying in bed with their heart pounding, paranoid they're going to die, just might cure them," Ricardo said.

"I'm serious," said Alex. "What should I say?"

BAD REACTIONS

"Let's talk about bad reactions," I said. "I promise I won't lie." I nodded toward Stephanie. "What kind of things can happen? What have you heard?"

"Like I said," Ricardo added, "your heart beats faster and you can get paranoid."

"Absolutely true," I said. "What else?"

"Eyes get red," Kate added.

"Mouth gets dry," said Bev.

"Can't think straight," said Elise.

"Eat too much," said Denise.

"All true," I said.

"But what do I say?" asked Alex.

"The point," I said, "is that it's not fun for everyone. A lot of people don't get high at all the first time they use."

"It just doesn't work?" asked Sebastian.

"They don't really know how to inhale," I said.

"So they can run for president," Kate joked.

"Plenty of people just don't like the effects. It's perfectly reasonable to tell your kids that," I said. "Marijuana makes some people disoriented and anxious. Their heart beats quickly and they panic. It hardly sounds like a good time."

"But their friends are all telling them it's great," Alex said. "Come on!"

"But it might not be great for them," Ricardo said.

"I don't think that's enough. I don't think that saying it's too strong or that it'll make them paranoid is going to keep my kids away." Alex folded his arms.

"I don't know that any one thing will do it." I nodded. "But there's more to it than just potency and paranoia."

"It sounds like from what you were saying, stronger pot is safer," said Sebastian.

"I think Alex's point is a good one. Stronger pot could certainly sneak up on inexperienced users. They could get alarmed. But as far as your lungs are concerned, stronger pot is safer. If you've got ditch weed and you need to smoke a whole gram to get high, you're exposing yourself to more smoke. In contrast, if one hit does the trick, then you're exposed to less smoke."

"Could we talk about the lung stuff?" asked Kate. "How many cigarettes equal one joint?"

"There's no time like the present," I said. "But would you like to take a break first?"

"Please!" they all said.

Most everyone stepped outside, but Alex approached me and said quietly, "I don't mean to fly off the handle or anything. This is hard stuff."

"This is hard stuff. I agree."

LUNG HEALTH AND CANCER

Everyone returned with sodas and chips. I went to the board and wrote "CIGARETTES" in big letters. "Cigarette smoking is down by leaps and bounds," I said. "How come?"

"Those things kill you!" Sebastian said.

"And everybody knows it," added Stephanie.

"You've got it. It's not news anymore. Cigarettes are still killing people. They're still the No. 1 cause of death—more than any other single cause. But word is out. How many of you still smoke?" A couple people raised their hands sheepishly. "I don't even have to tell you what to do. Come to my office if you want some coaching. You should be afraid of these things."

"But marijuana's even worse, right?" Denise asked.

"We've done such a good job of scaring everyone off cigarettes because they really are dangerous. Why not capitalize on all that work? Just hook marijuana to cigarettes and get the same fears going. Wouldn't everybody stop smoking pot if they knew it was more carcinogenic than cigarettes?"

"I guess so," said Bev. "It just doesn't seem right."

"You've seen the advertisements. How many cigarettes is a joint supposed to equal?"

"Four," Sebastian said.

"Four it is," I said. "So why aren't people jumping away four times as fast?"

"Cigarette smokers smoke like 20 a day," Stephanie said. "Nobody smokes 20 joints a day."

"Okay," I said. "But a joint is supposed to be the same as four cigarettes, so you'd only need five a day. Who smokes five joints a day?"

"Nobody I know," Sebastian said.

"That doesn't mean you're off the hook," I said. "A couple things keep coming up. People who smoke just one joint a day show respiratory symptoms. They cough up junk and wheeze and all of that."[38]

"That's not exactly lung cancer," said Alex.

"Yeah," Sebastian said. "I just heard something about marijuana not causing lung cancer."

"That's true," I said. "Don Tashkin from UCLA presented data from over 1,000 people and found that marijuana smoking didn't cause cancer. He was at the International Cannabinoid Research meeting, so the paper isn't out yet. Still, at least one study shows some changes in lung cells that look pre-cancerous.[39] There's also one study done very well that shows more head and neck cancers in pot smokers."[40]

"Those guys were probably smoking cigarettes, too," said Alex.

"It looks like cigarettes definitely make things worse," I said. "Stay away from those things. But marijuana smoke has plenty of nasty junk in it, too."

"What if you use a water pipe?" asked Denise. "I mean, what if somebody uses one?"

"Yeah, is a bong better than a joint?" Sebastian asked.

"We're getting into some drug-safety stuff that I think is really important," I said. "Look, I've gotten in a ton of trouble talking about this before. It didn't happen here and I don't want it to happen here. You can imagine."

"Don't make us beg," said Stephanie.

"Okay, the way to make sure you never get any lung damage from marijuana is to never smoke it. If your kids ask you what you learned today, tell them Dr. Earleywine told you to never smoke pot. Now what did I say?"

"Don't smoke pot," said Kate.

"There are a couple things to keep in mind about marijuana and lung health. First off, the steps you take to protect your lungs don't protect you against brain changes. They don't protect you against dependence or abuse, either. Understand? There are still other negative consequences of marijuana, especially for kids."

"Okay," said Stephanie. "We hear the warning."

"One thing that makes marijuana more dangerous is that people hold the smoke down in their lungs." I took a deep breath and held it, then motioned as if I was counting to myself. Then I pretended to cough.

"The lung buster!" said Ricardo.

"You don't need to do that," I said. "I know that everybody thinks they're getting the most for their money that way. All you're doing is giving the tars a better chance to deposit in your lungs."

"You get higher that way, though," said Alex.

"You do," I said. "But it's not because of the pot. I just got a head rush right there from holding my breath." A couple people laughed. "James Zacny at the University of Chicago showed that people got higher holding their breath even when they had the placebo weed. Holding 10 seconds didn't get anybody higher than just inhaling and exhaling, either."[41]

"For real?" asked Denise.

"Yes," I said. "So there's no reason to hold these giant hits all day. If you're dying to hold your breath to get a head rush, blow the smoke out first."

"That's funny. We used to do that in grade school," said Ada. "I mean, just hold your breath."

"I'm glad you weren't getting high in grade school," I said. "So don't hold hits. Now what about the water pipes?"

"It cools the smoke," said Sebastian.

"It does cool the smoke," I said. "And heat is hard on your lungs. Those little metal one-hitters people take to concerts are going to fry everybody's chests."

"If they don't burn your lip first," said Denise.

"Everybody had high hopes for the water pipes. No pun intended. But they're not ideal. The THC gets trapped in the water, so people end up smoking more than they would normally. That's what's good about the vaporizer."

"The what?" asked Bev.

"The vaporizer. The vaporizer is a gizmo that heats marijuana so the active ingredients boil off, but it never actually catches fire. The active ingredients come out in a fine mist. You never get exposed to carcinogens because there aren't any."[42]

"Cool," said Stephanie.

"I need to caution you, though. I've seen people turn some vaporizers up too high. The mist is supposed to be very fine. You can barely see it. Most people can't believe it, so they crank up the heat. It defeats the whole purpose. If you can see smoke, then it's not working right."

"Is it expensive?" asked Alex.

"It's cheaper than an iron lung," I said.

"What if you eat pot?" asked Stephanie.

"Yeah, what about brownies?" Bev asked.

"Obviously, if there's no fire, there's no smoke," I said. "You can't do lung damage with orally administered pot. Eating brownies can't hurt your respiratory system. But I have to caution you about watching your dosage."

"What do you mean?" asked Bev.

"People who are accustomed to smoking pot tend to expect rapid effects from eating pot, too. It takes a long time, up to three hours some-times, to get the full effects. Most people just aren't that patient."

"Hey!" said Bev.

"I mean it. People eat a brownie and wait half an hour and nothing happens. So they eat two more. Three hours later they're babbling about zombies. Then they get the munchies and guess what's handy?"

"More brownies!" Stephanie shouted.

"You said it. Then they're baked into next week. So eating pot helps your lungs, but watch out for the dosage. Don't hold your hits. Vaporize." I paused. "And by all means, stay away from those nasty cigarettes."

"It sounds more like you're talking to us than our kids," Alex said.

"You got it. Now that you know the impact on teen brains, I think you can all get the point across. But you all know users, even adults, who could benefit from this information."

Ada looked at her watch. "Time flies," she said.

"Do you all feel like you understand?" I asked. Everyone nodded.

"There are a few more things that might help you make the case with your teens, or at least make you sound like an authority on the matter. The first one concerns sperm count."

"Not the peanut testicles again," said Alex with a grin.

CHAPTER 12: SEX, LEGAL TROUBLES AND DRIVING

SPERM COUNT AND MOTILITY

"I don't want to insult Alex's gym teacher. I think he might have been mis-informed. There are some data on sperm count that he might have been thinking of."

"Marijuana just makes guys horny," said Ada. The women chuckled and the guys smiled.

"It's not that," I said. "Actually, data support that, too. But I mean count and motility. Sperm function doesn't have anything to do with desire. At least one study has shown that men who smoke daily have lower sperm count and motility.[43] Instead of swimming fast," I said, moving my hand through the air quickly, "they swim slower." I moved my hand through the air slowly. "Get it?"

"I hope not!" said Sebastian.

"This isn't birth control!" I said. "I'm not kidding, either. The first study showed decreased counts but they didn't go below normal levels. It only takes one sperm to get somebody pregnant. Believe me."

SAFE SEX

"Speaking of horny," said Ada. "What about safe sex?"

"I'm not talking about horny!" I said. "But it's a good question. I don't want your kids leaving crazy messages on my phone." Everyone just sat. "I know you all have never had sex." I smiled. "And you don't want to think about your kids doing it."

"Don't get me started," said Stephanie.

"So the safe-sex and drug-use research is a mess. There are links between marijuana and unsafe sex. It's hard to tell if marijuana actually makes people lousy at putting on a condom or if people who hate con-doms also happen to like smoking pot."[44]

"Whoa!" said Kate. "I don't even want to think about this."

"I've got two daughters myself," I said. "It's hard to fathom. Parents have to handle this one in their own way. But the same skills apply. Listening, asking questions when the opportunities arise."

"Not lecturing," added Stephanie.

"This is important with alcohol, too." I added. "Michael Carey and his team at Syracuse University got guys drunk and just asked them about their attitudes about condoms. After a couple of beers, men don't like condoms too much."[45]

"You're telling me!" said Bev.

"So it might be the same way with marijuana. It's not true in every case. But one study of men in England showed that if they had smoked marijuana within the two hours before having sex, they were less likely to use a condom. It's not clear exactly why."

"Maybe it's the lower IQ," Kate joked.

"My friend Barbara Leigh has shown that condom use is particularly bad the first time people have sex with a new partner. The bottom line is: Always have a condom around." I paused a minute. "I guess I don't need to waste my breath about telling your kids to wait until they're married."

"You sure don't," said Stephanie.

SIZE MATTERS

"Back to Alex's gym coach, though. There are data showing that teens who smoke pot don't grow as big. I don't know why the drug czar doesn't hit this harder," I said. "The data are pretty compelling. The same guys at Duke who showed that marijuana alters the gray and white matter of your brain also find this. Folks who started smoking in their teens ended up smaller than the folks who smoked later in life."

"You talking whole body or just parts?" asked Sebastian. The guys smiled.

"No," I said. "Weight and height. This might not sound important at first. But when you think about what it means and how this might happen, it's pretty haunting. The guys who started smoking early were three inches shorter than the guys who started later."

"Three inches!" said Alex. "That sounds like a lot."

"I don't mean to alarm the short guys. I'm only 5-foot-9 myself. But it's rough being short, especially in America. Think of all the expressions we have for how great it is to be tall."

"Like 'looked up to'?" asked Stephanie.

"Right," I said.

"And 'looked down on'!" added Ricardo.

"Big man on campus!" said Ada.

"How about 'stand tall'?" added Kate.

"Head and shoulders above the rest!" said Stephanie.

"Put on a pedestal," said Sebastian.

"Okay," I said. "You're good at this. As you can see, there's a lot of language glorifying height. The research suggests it's hard on men to be short. Tall men are more likely to have children. They're considered more persuasive. They have more self-esteem and tend to earn more money. I'm not saying it's fair. It's just how it is."

"That stinks," said Sebastian. "It's just not right."

"Adolescence is hard enough," I said. "No need to do anything that might slow down your growth."

"It sounds silly, though," said Kate. "That's what they used to tell us about cigarettes—that they'll stunt your growth. How would it do that?"

"We're not sure. Marijuana alters hormones in some folks, at least when they first start using. People seem to develop tolerance to it. But even a small change in hormones during a critical period like adolescence can mess up growth. The animal literature is clear on marijuana decreasing growth hormone, too."

"I just don't think my kids will believe that marijuana stunts your growth," said Alex.

"The data support it, though," I said. "It's just more information to add to the mix. It could be important for some teens and not for others. You know your kids better than I do."

"I don't see any harm throwing it in if it's true," Elise said.

"It just feels funny," said Kate. "Anyway, talk about the next thing."

"I don't want to run away from the feelings," I said. "How does it feel to think that marijuana might decrease growth?"

"It's not that big a deal," Kate said. "I just have to admit, it makes me wonder a little bit about myself." She ran a hand through her hair. "I don't mean to turn this into group therapy."

"Go ahead," said Stephanie.

"I played a lot of sports and I thought I might be up for a basketball scholarship when I applied to college. It's a long story, but it didn't happen." Kate stopped and frowned.

"So?" I asked.

"Who knows? If I'd been taller?"

"You've got a tale to tell your daughters now, though, don't you?" Stephanie asked.

"I guess so. I guess so." Kate sat up in her chair. "Anyway, let's finish up."

LEGAL PROBLEMS

"I only really have two other areas to cover," I said. "Driving and legal issues."

"Do the legal stuff first," said Elise. "I'm really worried about that."

"I'm not going to help your worrying," I said. "I don't want to sound like a cop. I also don't want to sound like some kind of paranoid pothead."

"A little late for that," said Stephanie with a grin. I had to smile myself.

"First off, teens are more likely than adults to get busted. Period."[46]

"Whoa!" Kate held up her hand. "What makes you say that?"

"At least half of marijuana-possession arrests involve people under 21," I said.

"Do you think that cops are gunning for kids or something?" Kate asked.

"Aren't they more likely to use in the first place?" asked Ricardo.

"I think that's part of it," I said. "Teens are more likely to buy from strangers. They're more likely to resell some of their marijuana. Both of those things increase the chance for arrest."

"So what's your point?" Ada asked.

"It's just that no teens think they're the ones who are going to get busted."

"They think they're immune," said Bev.

"Or they think they can tell a policeman a mile away," said Alex, shaking his head.

"Everybody thinks that," I said. "Until it's too late. I hate using the threat of a bust as a big reason for teens to stay away from marijuana, but it's true."

"What happens to them?" asked Elise.

"It depends on how much they have, doesn't it?" asked Sebastian.

"Every case is different," I said. "If there's a bigger amount, or a lot of cash around, or a million lunch baggies, or anything that looks like marijuana sales, things get very bad."

"I had a friend whose son got pulled over. He had pot and baggies, so they charged him with distribution," said Sebastian.

"What'd they do?" asked Stephanie.

"He ended up going to a treatment program," said Sebastian. "I'm not really even sure he got high very much."

"I bet it was expensive," Stephanie said.

"Out of this world," Sebastian said. "The treatment, the lawyer and the court fees put them in debt. I think they emptied out the college fund."

"Ow!" said Kate, grimacing.

"It can get much worse," I said. "If they're over 18 and it looks like they're selling to minors, it can mean jail time."

"Really?" asked Elise.

"When I left California, possessing a joint was a $100 fine or so. But an 18-year-old passing it to a 17-year-old is distributing to a minor. Three years to seven years in prison."

"Come on!" said Stephanie.

"I'm not making this up," I said. "A couple other things. Anyone busted near a school gets extra time added to any sentence. If you live near a school and get busted at home, then the extra jail time gets added automatically."

"No way!" said Elise.

"It's true," I said. "I assume I don't need to tell you about giving marijuana to your kids or their friends, or letting them party at your house."

"Tell us anyway," Stephanie said.

"A story might help," I said. "A lenient dad in Iowa let his sons bring their pals over to party. I guess he was trying to be cool. He apparently sold them grass."

"Uh-oh," said Kate.

"So it turned into child endangerment. It was also recruiting a minor into the drug trade since his sons brought the kids over."

"What'd he get?" Alex asked.

"Thirty-seven years." Everyone gasped. It seemed like the room was quiet for quite a few moments.

"He deserved it," Elise said. "I'm sorry. I know that some of you want to see the laws change, but I don't want anybody pushing any drugs on my kids." Everyone stayed quiet.

"I agree," I said. Elise looked surprised. "Nobody wants marijuana in the hands of minors. Every drug-reform group is on your side."

"I didn't realize that," Elise said softly.

"Seriously," I said. "They all argue that a controlled, taxed, regulated marijuana market has a better chance of keeping marijuana away from teens than the underground. I don't see a lot of dealers carding people before they sell."

"I don't know if I buy that argument," Elise said.

"My point is that there are extra legal risks for you and your teens if they're involved with marijuana."

"That's clear," Elise said.

"If they're growing plants in the basement or in a closet somewhere, you could lose your house."

"What?" asked Kate.

"It's the forfeiture laws," said Ricardo.

"What's the deal?" asked Sebastian.

"Basically," Ricardo began, "if your property looks like it's part of a crime or you bought it from money made from crime, then the police can take it."

"They can take your house for a plant?" Stephanie asked.

"If it looks like you bought the house with drug money," Ricardo said. "If you're driving a car full of dope, they can take the car, too."

"Whoa!" said Kate. "I don't even know what to say to that."

"The bottom line is that a couple of harmless plants can cost a lot," I said.

"I follow," said Ada. "This is really serious." The mood in the room was a little deflated.

"I didn't mean for this to turn into a big bummer," I said. "But it sends the message home. This stuff is important."

DRIVING

"I don't want to be the one running away from the feelings, but what's the word on driving?" asked Sebastian. "I know people who claim that marijuana doesn't have any effect on their driving."

"Me, too." I nodded.

"So what's the big deal?"

"My biggest concern is just that driving is dangerous no matter what. There are over 40,000 traffic deaths every year in the U.S."

"Not from marijuana," said Alex.

"No," I said. "That's the total. Over half of those people weren't wearing seatbelts."

"What goes through their minds?" asked Elise.

"At the last second," Ricardo said, "the thing going through their minds is probably 'I wish I'd worn my seatbelt.'"

"I thought there was some study in the Netherlands that said driving was okay," said Alex.

"I know the one you're thinking of," I said. "A guy named Robbe had people smoke and then drive around in Amsterdam with a driving instructor in the car."

"Remind me not to drive over there," said Kate.

"They did okay on the turns and handling. They actually drove slower and stayed away from other cars. They started putting on the brakes earlier when they have to stop, too. But they had trouble staying in the middle of the lane."[47]

"Were these teens?" asked Elise.

"Good question," I said. "No. We don't know that teens would do as well because they're still learning to drive. We also don't know how the people in the experiment would have done in an emergency situation."

"Not as well as if they weren't high," Elise said.

"Driving well with a driving instructor sitting right next to you isn't exactly the same thing as driving around by yourself," Ricardo said.

"Good point," said Stephanie.

"I agree," I said. "A lot of teens drive better with an adult in the car, but a lot of teen accidents happen when other teens are in the car."

"Don't remind me," Kate said.

"Another story to tell?" I asked.

"No thanks. I'd rather not relive it."

"I would really bust some heads for that," said Alex.

"I think that's part of the problem," said Stephanie. "No offense, Alex. I just mean that we threaten them with a whipping when really we're saying how sad we'd be if they got hurt."

"No kidding," Elise said.

"I know what you mean," said Alex. "Soft emotions and all that."

"What would it be like to tell your kids you loved them when they got in the car?" I asked. Nobody said a word.

"What do you mean?" asked Ricardo.

"You know," I said. "If your kid gets behind the wheel and you say 'Please wear your seatbelt and drive carefully because I love you and I don't want you to get hurt.'"

"I'd probably burst into tears," said Elise with a smile.

"It's easier to say 'Wear your seatbelt or I'll kick your butt.'" Ricardo grinned.

"I can hear my kids groaning," said Stephanie. "You know, 'Oh, Mom!'"

"I think they'd hear it, though," said Kate. "I know they'd tease me, but I think they'd hear me."

IN THE END

"I guess that's what it's all about, really," Stephanie said.

"The driving?" asked Alex.

"No, getting them to hear you."

"I never thought about it that way," Sebastian said. "We're kind of back to the first day."

"I hope you have more information now," I said. "All this health and lungs and laws and driving ought to count for something."

"Now you're the one running away from the feelings." Kate pointed right at me. I just shrugged.

"It's what you told me on the first day," Ada said. "Tell them that you love them."

"This is getting a little too sappy for me," Ricardo said.

"It is sappy, but you're right," I said, looking to Ada. "In the end, it's all about the love."

"We didn't spend all this time just to learn that love's important," Alex said.

"Of course not," I said. "We covered the myths about marijuana. There's really no gateway or amotivation or violence. There is concern about brain development in teens and brain function in any heavy user. We've got real concerns about driving, legal problems, messing up in school and getting dependent, too."

"Yes," said Stephanie. "But it's how we get it across."

"I agree," I said. "Remember to listen, to reflect, to talk about feelings, to let them experience their feelings. What else?"

"Don't lecture," said Kate. "Look for opportunities."

"Let them talk," said Elise.

"I just like the love part," said Ada. "That I can handle."

"I think you folks can handle it all," I said. "Don't hesitate to call me or send an e-mail if things get rough. I had a good time. Hope you did, too." I waved.

"Thanks a lot," said Ada as she left.

"Yes, thanks!" said Stephanie.

Alex lingered as the others left. I didn't want to grill him, but I wondered how it went.

"So?" I asked.

"I did it," he said. "I don't want to make a big deal out of it, but I did it."

"It is a big deal," I said. "That's great. How'd it work?"

"Just putting the vaporizer away does it. I'm not saying I got it licked, but it was really not much effort."

"How do you feel?"

"Happy. That's a feeling word, right? I'm happy and I'm proud of myself. I feel funny making so much of it, but it's nice."

"Think you can keep it going?"

"Without a doubt."

"What makes you think so?"

"I'm just noticing little differences. I used to watch TV all high. Now I watch it straight and realize I hate most of it. I'm reading more, like I said."

"Great."

"I still really enjoy it when I do get high. There's something to be said for that."

"I agree," I said.

"But I actually enjoy it more. It's more of an event. It's special again. I can't quite explain it. It's just special again."

"How's your girlfriend handling it?"

"Ha! She still doesn't believe it. I think she's afraid to get too excited about it for fear I'll go back to the old ways."

"Do you think there's anything that would make you go back?"

"Maybe when the kids are in college or something. If I could do it without feeling like a hypocrite. But by then, who knows what I'll be doing."

"You mentioned you use it as a reward. Are there special events or goals coming up where you might want to use?"

"There are," Alex said. "But I just plan ahead for them. I make that my night for the week. I've got a big project at work, and the day we turn it over to the client is definitely going to be my day. But I'll know a long time ahead of time. I'll just make that night be my one for the week."

"I understand," I said.

"Yes, I think you do." Alex nodded. "Thanks."

"Tell you what," I said. "Give me a call at the end of the month no matter how you're doing. If things slip up, we can talk about it. If things are fine, we can enjoy that, too."

"Will do," Alex said, extending his hand. We shook on it. "I'm going to do all this stuff. I promise." He headed out the door. I sat in the empty room a minute. It was quiet with everybody gone. I'll never know how everything will turn out for all these people and all their children. But at that moment, I had a lot of hope.

FOOTNOTES

[1] See "How Effective Is Drug Abuse Resistance Education? A Meta-Analysis of Project DARE Outcome Evaluations," by Ennett, Susan; Tobler, Nancy; Ringwalt, Christopher; Flewelling, Robert. In *American Journal of Public Health*, Vol. 84(9), September 1994, 1394–1401.

[2] See "Interpersonal Contributors to Drug Use: The Willing Host," by Newcomb, Michael; Earleywine, Mitchell. In *American Behavioral Scientist*, Vol. 39(7), June 1996, 823–837.

[3] See "Project DARE: No Effects at 10-Year Follow-Up," by Lynam, Donald R.; Milich, Richard; Zimmerman, Rick; Novak, Scott P.; Logan, T.K.; Martin, Catherine; Leukefeld, Carl; Clayton, Richard. In *Journal of Consulting and Clinical Psychology*, Vol. 67(4), August 1999, 590–593.

[4] See "Good Reasons for Ignoring Good Evaluation: The Case of the Drug Abuse Resistance Education (D.A.R.E.) Program," by Birkeland, Sarah; Murphy-Graham, Erin; Weiss, Carol. In *Evaluation and Program Planning*, Vol. 28(3), August 2005, 247–256.

[5] See "Stages of Drug Use: A Community Survey of Perth Teenagers," by Blaze-Temple, Debra; Lo, Sing Kai. In *British Journal of Addiction*, Vol. 87(2), February 1992, 215–225; also "The Shifting Importance of Alcohol and Marijuana as Gateway Substances Among Serious Drug Abusers," by Golub, Andrew; Johnson, Bruce D. In *Journal of Studies on Alcohol*, Vol. 55(5), September 1994, 607–614; and "Sequence of Drug Use Among Serious Drug Users: Typical vs. Atypical Progression," by Mackesy-Amiti, Mary-Ellen; Fendrich, Michael; Goldstein, Paul J. In *Drug and Alcohol Dependence*, Vol. 45(3), May 1997, 185–196.

[6] See "Heavy Caffeine Use and the Beginning of the Substance Use Onset Process: An Illustration of Latent Transition Analysis," by Collins, Linda M.; Graham, John W.; Rousculp, Susannah Scarborough; Hansen, William B. In K. Bryant, M. Windle, & S. West (Eds.), *The Science of Prevention: Methodological Advances From Alcohol and Substance Abuse Research* (pp.79–99), 1997, Washington, D.C., American Psychological Association.

[7] See "The Association Between Cigarette Smoking and Drug Abuse in the United States," by Lai, Shenghan; Lai, Hong; Page, Bryan J.; McCoy, Clyde B. In *Journal of Addictive Diseases*, Vol. 19(4), 2000, 11–24.

[8] See "Loss of Control Drinking in Alcoholics: An Experimental Analogue," by Marlatt, G. Alan; Demming, Barbara; Reid, John B. In *Journal of Abnormal Psychology*, Vol. 81(3), June 1973, 233–241.

[9] See "The Effects of Marijuana on Human Physical Aggression," by Myerscough, Rodney; Taylor, Stuart P. In *Journal of Personality and Social Psychology*, Vol. 49(6), December 1985, 1541–1546.

[10] See "Alcohol, Marijuana, Hard Drugs and Aggression: A Structural Equation Modeling Analysis," by Denson, Thomas; Earleywine, Mitchell (under review).

[11] See "Acute Effects of Marijuana Smoking on Aggressive, Escape and Point-Maintained Responding of Male Drug Users," by Cherek, Don R.; Roache, John D.; Egli, Mark; Davis, Chester. In *Psychopharmacology*, Vol. 111(2), May 1993, 163–168.

[12] See "Alcohol's Effect on Triggered Displaced Aggression," by Aviles, Fredy; Earleywine, Mitchell; Pollock, Vicki; Stratton, Joy; Miller, Norman. In *Psychology of Addictive Behaviors*, Vol. 19(1), March 2005, 108–111.

[13] See "How Do Genes Influence Marijuana Use? The Role of Subjective Effects," by Lyons, Michael J.; Toomey, Rosemary; Meyer, Joanne M.; Green, Alan I.; Eisen, Seth A.; Goldberg, Jack; True, William R.; Tsuang, Ming T. In *Addiction*, Vol. 92(4), April 1997, 409–417.

[14] See *Diagnostic and Statistical Manual of Mental Disorders* (*DSM-IV-TR*), American Psychiatric Association, Fourth Edition, 1994, Washington, D.C.

[15] See "Cannabis, Motivation, and Life Satisfaction in an Internet Sample," by Smucker Barnwell, Sara; Earleywine, Mitchell; Wilcox, Rand. In *Substance Abuse Treatment, Prevention, and Policy*, Vol. 1, 2006, 1–9.

[16] See "Chronic Marijuana Use and Psychosocial Adaptation," by Hochman, Joel S.; Brill, Noman Q. In *American Journal of Psychiatry*, Vol. 130(2), February 1973, 132–139.

[17] See "Correlates of Marijuana Use Among College Students," by Gergen, Mary K.; Gergen, Kenneth J.; Morse, Stanley J. In *Journal of Applied Social Psychology*, Vol. 2(1), January 1972, 1–16; also "The Use of Marijuana and Other Illegal Drugs on a College Campus," by Goode, Erich. In *British Journal of Addiction to Alcohol and Other Drugs*, Vol. 66(4), December 1971, 335–336.

[18] See "The Effects of Drug Use on the Wages of Young Adults," by Kaestner, Robert. In *Journal of Labor Economics*, Vol. 9, 1991, 381–412; also "The Effect of Illicit Drug Use on the Labor Supply of Young Adults," by Kaestner, Robert. In *Journal of Human Resources*, Vol. 29, 1994, 123–136; and "New Estimates of the Effect of Marijuana and Cocaine on Wages: Accounting for Unobserved Person Specific Effects," by Kaestner, Robert. In *Industrial and Labor Relations Review*, Vol. 47, 1994, 454–470.

[19] See "Motivation Levels and the Marihuana High," by Pihl, R. O.; Sigal, H. In *Journal of Abnormal Psychology*, Vol. 87(2), April 1978, 280–285.

[20] See "An Experimental Study of the Effects of Daily Cannabis Smoking on Behavior Patterns," by Miles, C. G.; Congreve, G. R. S.; Gibbins, R. J.; Marshman, J.; Devenyi, P.; Hicks, R. C. In *Acta Pharmacologica et Toxicologica*, Vol. 34 (Suppl. 7), 1–43.

[21] See "Performance on a Verbal Learning Task by Subjects of Heavy Past Marijuana Usage," by Cohen, Michael J.; Rickles, William H. In *Psychopharmacologia*, Vol. 37(4), 1974, 323–330.

[22] See "The Effects of Adolescent Cannabis Use on Educational Attainment: A Review," by Lynskey, Michael; Hall, Wayne. In *Addiction*, Vol. 95(11), November 2000, 1621–1630.

[23] See "Reducing Heavy Drinking in College Males with the Decisional Balance: Analyzing an Element of Motivational Interviewing," by LaBrie, Joseph W.; Pedersen, Eric R.; Earleywine, Mitchell; Olsen, Hutson. In *Addictive Behaviors*, Vol. 31(2), February 2006, 254–263.

[24] See "Brain Morphological Changes and Early Marijuana Use: A Magnetic Resonance and Positron Emission Tomography Study," by Wilson, William; Mathew, Roy;

Turkington, Timothy; Hawk, Thomas; Coleman, R. Edward; Provenzale, James. In *Journal of Addictive Diseases*, Vol. 19(1), 2000, 1–22.

[25] See "Altered Brain Tissue Composition in Heavy Marijuana Users," by Matochik, John A.; Eldreth, Dana A.; Cadet, Jean Lud; Bolla, Karen I. In *Drug And Alcohol Dependence*, Vol. 77(1), January 2005, 23–30.

[26] See "Effects of Chronic Marijuana Use on Human Cognition," by Block, Robert I.; Ghoneim, M. M. In *Psychopharmacology*, Vol. 110(1-2), January 1993, 219–228.

[27] See "Marijuana: Effects on Pulse Rate, Subjective Estimates of Intoxication and Multiple Measures of Memory," by Miller, Loren; Cornett, Teresa; Wikler, A. In *Life Sciences*, Vol. 25, 1979, 1325–1350.

[28] See "Acute Marijuana Effects on rCBF and Cognition: A PET study," by O'Leary D. S. In *Neuroreport*, Vol. 11(17), November 2000, 3835–3841.

[29] See "Increased Susceptibility to Memory Intrusions and the Stroop Interference Effect During Acute Marijuana Intoxication," by Hooker, William D.; Jones, Reese T. In *Psychopharmacology*, Vol. 91(1), January 1987, 20–24.

[30] See *Cannabis and Cognitive Functioning*, by Solowij, Nadia, 1998, New York: Cambridge University Press.

[31] See "Frontal Lobe Dysfunction in Long-Term Cannabis Users," by Lundqvist, T.; Jönsson, S.; Warkentin, S. In *Neurotoxicology and Teratology*, Vol. 23(5), September-October 2001, 437–443.

[32] See "Acute Marijuana Effects on rCBF and Cognition: A PET Study," by O'Leary, D. S.; Block, R.I.; Flaum, M.; Schultz, S. K.; Boles, Ponto L. L.; Watkins, G. L.; Hurtig, R. R.; Andreasen, N. C.; Hichwa, R. D. In *Neuroreport*, Vol. 11(17), November 2000, 3835–3841.

[33] See "Compensatory Responses to Placebo Vary with Presumed Personality 'Risk' for Alcoholism and Drinking Habits," by Earleywine, Mitchell; Finn, Peter R. In *International Journal of the Addictions*, Vol. 29(5), April 1994, 583–591.

[34] See "Childhood IQ and All-Cause Mortality Before and After Age 65: Prospective Observational Study Linking the Scottish Mental Survey 1932 and the Midspan Studies," by Hart, Carol L.; Taylor, M. D.; Smith, G. Davey; Whalley, L. J.; Starr, J. M.; Hole, D. J.; Wilson, V.; Deary, I. J. In *British Journal of Health Psychology*, Vol. 10(2), May 2005, 153–165; and "Quality of Life in Healthy Old Age: Relationships with Childhood IQ, Minor Psychological Symptoms and Optimism," by Bain, Gillian H.; Lemmon, Helen; Teunisse, Saskia; Starr, John M.; Fox, Helen C.; Deary, Ian J.; Whalley, Lawrence J. In *Social Psychiatry and Psychiatric Epidemiology*, Vol. 38(11), November 2003, 632–636.

[35] See "Neurocognitive Consequences of Marijuana—A Comparison with Pre-Drug Performance," by Fried, P.; Watkinson, B.; Gray, R. In *Neurotoxicology and Teratology*, Vol. 27(2), March-April 2005, 231–239.

[36] See "Moderation of the Effect of Adolescent-Onset Cannabis Use on Adult Psychosis by a Functional Polymorphism in the Catechol-O-Methyltransferase Gene: Longitudinal Evidence of a Gene X Environment Interaction,"

by Caspi, Avshalom; Moffit, Terrie E.; Cannon, Mary; McClay, Joseph; Murray, Robin; Harrington, HonaLee; Taylor, Alan; Arsenault, Louise; Williams, Ben; Braithwaite, Antony; Poulton, Richie; Craig, Ian W. In *Biological Psychiatry*, Vol. 57(10), May 2005, 1117–1127.

[37] See "Effects of Varying Marijuana Potency on Deposition of Tar and Delta9-THC in the Lung During Smoking," by Matthias, P.; Tashkin, D. P.; Marques-Magallanes, J. A.; Wilkins, J. N.; Simmons, M. S. In *Pharmacology, Biochemistry and Behavior*, Vol. 58, 1997, 1145–1150.

[38] See "Respiratory Symptoms and Lung Function in Habitual, Heavy Smokers of Marijuana Alone, Smokers of Marijuana and Tobacco, Smokers of Tobacco Alone, and Nonsmokers," by Tashkin, D. P.; Coulson, A. H.; Clark, V. A.; Simmons, M.; Bourque, L. B.; Duann, S.; Spivey, G. H.; Gong, H. In *American Review of Respiratory Disease*, Vol. 135, 1987, 209–216.

[39] See "Endobronchial Injury in Young Tobacco and Marijuana Smokers as Evaluated by Visual, Pathologic and Molecular Criteria," by Roth, M. D.; Kleerup, E. C.; Arora, A.; Barsky, S. H.; Tashkin, D. P. In *American Journal of Respiratory and Critical Care Medicine*, Vol. 153, 1996, 100A.

[40] See "Marijuana Smoking and Head and Neck Cancer," by Hashibe, Mia; Ford, D. E.; Zhang, Zou Feng. In *Journal of Clinical Pharmacology*, Vol. 42 (11 Supp.), November 2002, 103S–107S.

[41] See "Response to Marijuana as a Function of Potency and Breathhold Duration," by Zacny, James P.; Chait, L. D. In *Psychopharmacology*, Vol. 103(2), February 1991, 223–226.

[42] See "Evaluation of a Vaporizing Device (Volcano) for the Pulmonary Administration of Tetrahydrocannabinol," by Hazekamp, A. et al. In *Journal of Pharmaceutical Sciences*, Vol. 95, 2006, 1308–1317.

[43] See "Changes in Human Spermatozoa Associated with High-Dose Marijuana Smoking," by Hembree, W. C.; Nahas, G. G.; Zeidenberg, P.; Huang, H. F. S. In *Marijuana: Biological Effects, Analysis, Metabolism, Cellular Responses*, by Nahas, G. G.; Paton, W. D. M. (Eds.), 1979, 429–439, New York: Pergamon.

[44] See "Substance Use and Unsafe Sex Amongst Homosexual Men in Edinburgh," by Clutterbuck, D. J.; Gorman, D.; McMillan, A.; Lewis, R.; Macintyre, C. C. In *AIDS Care*, Vol. 13(4), August 2001, 527–35.

[45] See "Alcohol's Effects on Requisites for Sexual Risk Reduction in Men: An Initial Experimental Investigation," by Gordon, Christopher M.; Carey, Michael P. In *Health Psychology*, Vol. 15(1), January 1996, 56–60.

[46] See "Crimes of Indiscretion," by Gettman, J. B. 2005. Washington D.C.: NORML (http://www.norml.org/index.cfm?Group_ID=6411).

[47] See "Marijuana's Impairing Effects on Driving Are Moderate When Taken Alone but Severe When Combined with Alcohol," by Robbe, H. In *Human Psychopharmacology: Clinical and Experimental*, Vol. 13 (Suppl. 2), November 1998, S70–S78.